An Independent & Comprehensive Guide for Authors Wishing to Publish Their Own Books

(but not a guide to self-publishing)

An
Independent &
Comprehensive Guide
for Authors Wishing to Publish
Their Own Books

(But Not a Guide to Self-Publishing)

Peter Rogers

An Independent & Comprehensive Guide
for Authors Wishing to Publish Their Own Books

(But not a Guide to Self-Publishing)

Peter Rogers

ISBN 978 1900307 437

Published by
PORTAL
6 Forest Avenue, Peverel, Plymouth, PL2 3QD

CONTENTS

INTRODUCTION

So why not simply call this book some variation of, *a guide to self-publishing*?

There are several answers. The first is that the term *self-publishing*, within the industry, has developed a number of negative connotations that it is best to avoid.

Another problem is there are a great many guides to self-publishing to choose from and many of these are available absolutely free. The problem is that these guides are commonly produced by companies that want to sell you their book publishing service and are designed to show how easy it is to self-publish, using the service they provide while glossing over the potential risks and problems.

This book is independently produced and has no such connection or vested interest in any such company. Any business or service mentioned in this book is purely there to inform, thus enabling you to choose the most effective method of publication, nothing more. But more importantly, this book explains the criteria to use in making that decision on how to produce your book, which format and methodology to use.

To do this it is necessary to cover every aspect of the process, warts and all, explaining the different options available along with the pitfalls you may encounter along the way. Therefore this book is as comprehensive as it can be, explaining each option and covering the main points of each element of the process to provide enough information for any author to publish their own book, or decide they have more work to do before going ahead.

Much of the information in this book is based on, not only my own experiences as a writer, but also as someone who has worked for a major publishing imprint and for a small press publisher, before becoming an independent publisher with near 50 published titles, both my own and for other authors.

Unlike other *free* guides on the subject, the purpose of this book is to outline the pitfalls and the hurdles, because if you know where there is a pit, you can avoid it and if you know where there is a hurdle, you can jump it.

Publishing your own book is a relatively simple task; the trick is to do it properly. This book will try to show you how.

AVOIDING THE VANITY TRAP

So you have written a book and started your collection of rejection slips, getting to the point where self-publishing seems to be the only option. Then you see a host of advertisements from companies offering to publish your book, for a fee, all denying that they are the dreaded vanity press.

A hunter sets a trap to catch their prey, but even wild animals aren't so stupid as to walk into an obvious trap. So the trap is disguised and hidden so it can't be seen for what it is. And then this trap is baited, to lure in the prey. But a lot of authors are just so hungry to see their book in print that the idea they may be waling into a trap doesn't cross their mind. Or if it does, they dismiss any concern because of the promises being made.

No vanity publisher will ever admit that this is what they are, which begs the question, how do you identify a vanity publisher?

The nature of the vanity publishing is often misconstrued as being something driven by the vanity of the author. The author, driven by continued rejection but certain that their manuscript is as good as any written by any mainstream author, becomes determined to prove all those editors that rejected their manuscript are wrong. The problem is that there are many reasons for a manuscript to be rejected, a number of which have nothing to do with the quality of the story or the writing.

The story may have a good and original plot, remembering that King Nebuchadnezzar, back in Old Testament times, said 'There is nothing new under the sun.' The story may be better written than others already in print. Editors aren't infallible, but the reasons for rejection are many and varied and many once rejected authors have gone on to great success. In fact it is rare to find a successful author that hasn't suffered the pain and disappointment of continued rejection. We're they vain to continue fighting to prove they were right all along?

The fact is that vanity publishing has nothing whatsoever to do with the author's vanity or self-belief in the fact that they have written a great book. It is something an author should believe, while also accepting that any manuscript, however great, can be improved by judicious editing.

What is Vanity Publishing?

Within the publishing industry, Vanity Publishing is a technical term with a specific meaning that is understood by every aspect of that industry, from publishing house, to distribution, to each and every bookstore across the land.

To explain this it is necessary to understand the widget principle according to the theory of business modelling.

In business modelling, the *widget* is a generic term for the end product or service that any business intends to provide. For a farmer growing cabbages, the widget is those cabbages. For a car manufacturer, the widget is the cars they produce. In mainstream publishing the end product, the product they bring to market and from which they derive their profit, or loss, is a book. Therefore the *book,* according to the business model of any mainstream publisher can be referred to as a *widget,* or vice versa.

The difference is that in Vanity Publishing, the product from which they derive their profit is not by selling any book they may produce. The profit in the business model for any Vanity Publisher comes from the service they provide. This service is to publish books, any book no matter how good or bad the story, or how good or bad the quality of writing, or any other measure of literary merit. Therefore, according to the principle of business modelling, the *widget* in Vanity Publishing, from which they derive their main avenue of profit, is the service they provide, which is publishing books for a fee.

The more books they can publish the larger their profit margin and to a large extent, it doesn't matter whether they sell a single book. In fact the act of bringing a book to market, distribution and delivery along with the need to offer retail discounts, actually adds a cost that can detract from their bottom line profit. Vanity publishers make more money by not selling books, though modern technology, print of demand systems, e-books etc., have decreased some of these additional costs. New technology also makes it easier to create the illusion of selling, or at least advertising these books for sale through some website or other. That said, you still will not see any book by any vanity publisher on the shelf of any mainstream bookstore.

How to Identify a Vanity Publisher.

During the early days of printing, before publishing became a business, most individuals paid to have their books printed. Even famous writers like Charles Dickens paid to have their early works printed, often in serial form, a chapter at a time, the sale of enough copies of the first chapter paying for the printing of the second and so on. If sales fell away, so would publication of further chapters.

This is not Vanity Publishing as it was the common practice of the time. Even today, paying to have your book produced is not automatically Vanity Publishing. Even mainstream publishers pay a printer to produce the books they want to publish. The key difference is all the ancillary elements around the process, which will be covered step by step over the following chapters.

Prior to the advent of modern digital book production, the majority of books were produced using a lithographic printing system, though even this has evolved from the days of hot metal to the production of photo-ready artwork. This image, made from a polymer coating applied to a plastic or metal plate, can be printed directly from the plate, or offset, giving the name, offset litho printing.

This system, despite a number of various advances, requires a minimum print run of 1,000 copies to be viable and many printers still view this as being barely cost effective. However, printing isn't the only task to undertake when producing a book.

What follows is print finishing, which includes collating, folding, binding and trimming, all of which are time consuming processes that incur their own set up time before using the tools required to complete these processes. In business, time is money. In addition, a stack of 1,000 finished books will take up a considerable amount of space and no printer wants a stack of finished product cluttering up their storage space. This is not a problem for a genuine publisher because they also don't want a stack of unsold books cluttering up their warehouse. They want this book out on the shelf where the buying public can see and hopefully buy that book. The rule is that you can't sell a book unless you have a book to sell.

However, Vanity Publishers are not in the business of selling books. They are in the business of publishing books and it matters not a jot whether or not have any potential of finding a customer. To cut costs and maximise profit a Vanity Publisher would often include what is called, '*a Pulping Clause*' in whatever agreement they require you to sign.

Remember that any such agreement is, in business terms, a contract. More than that, it is a publishing contract and like any contract, you need to read and understand the meaning of every clause and notation that is included in the small print of that contract.

A typical vanity publisher contract will state, in large print, that your book will be printed and you (the author) will receive a minimum of 6 or maybe 12 finished books. Want any more and you will have to pay, despite that you've already paid to have your book produced. The contract will then state that to save **you** additional expense, the remaining 990 or so copies will be left unbound, to be bound and distributed in response to orders received.

This all sounds very good and beneficial except for the pulping clause tucked away somewhere in the small print. The pulping clause is a device that states that if any printed but unbound books remain after twelve months (or some other stated period) the author must then stump up some additional storage fee and if they don't do this, these unfolded, unbound, untrimmed but printed folio sheets will be sold for pulping.

This all sounds very green and friendly to the environment (recycling used paper is not new), until you consider that this unmarked paper, apart from the printing, is still in folio size sheets, with no glued edges, no waste trimmings. This means that from a recycling point of view, this is prime quality waste paper therefore worth more than if they were trimmed and glued into a finished book.

Now remember that the Vanity Publisher has already saved themselves the cost of collating, folding, binding and trimming what the author has paid for into a finished book. Now they make even more money from selling this paper for recycling. The author will not see a penny of this money. For a Vanity Publisher, it pays not to sell the books they are paid to produce.

Now remember that you cannot sell a book unless you have a book to sell. You can advertise and promote, but the selling aspect of marketing requires that you must have a book to sell. As a publisher's agent, I would walk into a bookshop or book distributor with sample copies of the books I wanted to sell. As an independent publisher in my own right, I still do this and despite all the new technology and modern distribution methods, it still works.

To a large extent new technology has made the pulping clause obsolete, though it can still be found hidden in some Vanity Publisher contracts. The modern version of the pulping clause is, in some cases, is the system called, Print On Demand.

The idea with POD (Print of Demand) is that the author receives the initial half dozen printed and bound copies. Further copies are then printed and bound, one at a time, as orders are received. The pages aren't even printed, so there is no need for a pulping clause. Nor is there any storage cost, other than gigabytes of computer memory. However, POD systems do not take away the cost factor of printing and print finishing and it can be argued that pure print on demand adds to these costs.

To print one book the operator first needs to access the correct file and then wait for the printing process to be completed. The pages should come out of the printer ready formatted so this saves that cost. Then the cover has to be printed and folded. The book will then need binding and maybe the binding machine, depending on format, will incur some set up time. The act of producing one book at a time, on demand, incurs a time penalty at each step of the process. Time is money and this time penalty increases the per book cost of any book produced using this method. The result is that books marketed using the POD system are often much more expensive than standard litho printed books.

Plus, you still won't have a physical book, in your

hand, to offer for sale.

That said, the technology used to produce individual books on demand does offer the benefit that it enables a publisher to produce books in smaller batches than required using a litho based process, but more than one at a time. For example, I use this method to produce books in print runs of 50 or 100 copies at a time. This gives me a small stock with which to fulfil orders as they arrive without needing to go through the process of set up and print, set up and bind, set up and trim, for each and every single book. The result is a more viable per book cost, therefore more viable selling price, which, as will be made clear further on, is an important aspect in selling the books you publish. Plus, if I didn't think I could sell at least 50 copies of a title I wouldn't bother.

An Eye on Sales

In 2008 the New York Times published an investigative article revealing the sales figures for a major 'we will publish your book' company. Their total sales turnover reached 2.5 million, but a breakdown of these figures revealed an average sales level of just 54 books per title. Obviously some authors have higher sales than others, but with an average of 54 copies per title, some authors will be lucky to have sold a single copy.

Records from another such company reveals that they have 23,000 authors producing 23,500 titles. The reason new and unknown authors find it difficult to find a publisher is that mainstream publishers make their profit from the sale of the books they publish. This means that they prefer to publish a second, third and so on new book by an established author with a proven following than a book by a new and unknown author. Mainstream publishers produce 5, 10, 20 and more titles per author. Estimates for the number of novels by the author Stephen King range upwards of 47 novels, plus a number of short story anthologies.

This record of 23,500 titles by 23,000 different authors tells its own story. Part of this story is that a maximum of 500 authors have come back to publish a second manuscript and this may be less because a few successful authors may have three or four books in the works. Any serious author will surely produce more than one book.

This relates to the infinite monkey theorem that, if you give a thousand monkeys a thousand typewriters you'll get the works of Shakespeare. Out of 23,000 authors you are bound to get some genuinely good books. As for the rest, the company has made a profit simply by publishing all those books, whether they sell or not.

Calculate this another way and the result is a speculative success rate of just over 2%. No business could survive if it only sold 2% of the products it produced.

Another company counts a book as a best seller when it achieves a sales volume of 500 copies. Compare this to the Sunday Times best seller list where Dan Brown's Angels & Demons has sold 39 million, or Stephen King's Dark Tower, 30 million. Genuine publishers set an annual sales target for their books running into thousands, yet one major publisher that advertises to publish your book for a fee, has a sales target of just 100 copies.

Look a bit deeper and consider the temptation of 80% royalties. You pay to have your book published and it is put on sale at £6.99 and if you're lucky, you achieve this sales target of 100 copies. This gives you royalties of £559.20, but you may have paid up to or over £1,000 to have your book published.

In another case, a certain P.O.D. Service charged a set up fee of £800. Each book ordered is then subject to further production cost (see above), leaving you £2.88 royalties for each copy sold. Again you're lucky and reach this 100 books sales target. So for an investment of £800 you have a return of £288. You might actually show a profit in three or four years, but only if you ignore the other statistic, an average sale of 54 books per title.

Additional Marketing Fees

All genuine publishers want to sell the books they publish. This is, after all, how they make their money.

Marketing is therefore part of the cost of production. It is included from the very beginning of the process. When deciding to publish, a mainstream publisher will consider how much it will cost to promote and market this book and include it in all their calculations. Another reason for rejection with new authors.

Vanity Publishers aren't worried about marketing, other than it provides them with something else they can charge for. So they charge to publish your book and then sell additional marketing services, all with no guarantee of achieving results, but if you don't pay these extra fees they'll argue that you can't really complain if you haven't sold any copies of the book you've paid them to produce.

Vanity Publishing is a business that gains its income and profits from the fee it charges to publish a book, whether or not they sell a single copy of that book. Genuine publishing is a business that gains its income and profit from selling the books it publishes.

I repeat, no Vanity Publisher will ever admit that this is what they are. They disguise themselves, but the one thing they all do is stick up a big sign saying, 'We will publish your book.'

Whatever you do, avoid the vanity trap.

A QUESTION OF HATS

It is commonly said that an author cannot properly self-edit their own writing, that whatever else they intend to do themselves, an author should always employ someone else to edit their manuscript. The reasons are many and varied, but it all boils down to headology, psychology if you like, or a question of hats.

The term hat in this context is a figurative expression dating back to the time when person's job and social status could be identified by the type of hat they wore. The ordinary worker would be identified by the fact that they wore a flat cap. Middle management would wear a trilby hat while anyone in senior management would wear a bowler hat. Anyone daring to wear a hat above their status would suffer the consequences, sometimes even dismissal, simply for wearing the wrong hat. So, a sailor wears a sailors hat, a banker wears a bankers hat and a writer wears a writers hat and an editor, wears the hat of an editor, figuratively speaking.

In short, a writer looks at a manuscript from the perspective of a writer and all too often, when trying to edit, start re-writing as they go. An editor looks at a manuscript in a completely way from how a writer looks at a manuscript. It is also a completely different way from how the final reader looks at a book, but this is another issue. Figuratively speaking, to edit their own work, a writer must be able to take off their writer's hat and put on the hat of an editor and the same applies to self-publishing.

The problem is that writers that self-publish often do so wearing their writer's hat and therefore fail to see the pitfalls and hurdles they need to cross to achieve success. Consider the situation.

For the writer, continued rejection without explanation often creates a level of frustration that can supersede rational consideration of a manuscript's real potential. This is a perfectly natural and understandable reaction because writers are artists. Writers are as creative and driven as any painter or sculptor, or anyone producing any other form of creative art. A painter or sculptor though, can take their finished piece of art and hold an exhibition, or place it in one of the many art shops that display works for sale on a commission basis.

The writer cannot do this because they produce a manuscript and a manuscript is the raw material that needs to be converted into book form before it can be sold. All this makes the frustrated writer a prime target for the vultures in the industry, vanity publishers and the like. Then along comes new technology, digital formatting, e-books, print on demand, and so on, all making it easier for any author to self-publish.

There is a common quip among publishers, attributed to the influential journalist, Christopher Hitchens that, *'Everyone has a book in them and that, in most cases, this is where it should stay.'*

In most cases, this is where these book remain, or if laboriously written on some old typewriter, the manuscript then languishes in the bottom draw of whoever wrote it never to see the light of day again. The advent of new technology means that such manuscripts can now be uploaded and turned into e-books, often at virtually no cost whatsoever.

Consider this. The writer, looking at publishing from an author's perspective, wearing their writer's hat, commonly looks at the advent of e-books as a good thing. E-publishing makes it easy for them to self-publish and get their book out there, and once out there, they believe their book is virtually guaranteed to sell.

The publisher, wearing their publisher's hat, looks at the advent of e-books as yet another obstacle to selling the book they intend to publish. Every other book out in the market simply adds to the competition their book needs to compete with to achieve sales. Because of this new technology, absolutely anyone can publish a book, even those books that should have remained where they were, buried in the mind or bottom draw of all those people that have a book in them, which is where it should remain.

Of course this new technology also provides an

opportunity for good writers and good books that otherwise might not see the light of day to achieve a place in the market. But it also increases the level of dross those good books need to struggle through to get noticed.

You make think this harsh, but it is no less true.

The key issue here is that a writer will approach the process of turning their manuscript into a book as a writer. They will self-publish. A publisher will approach the same process from the perspective of a publisher, which is something completely different.

So here's a question. Can you look at your own manuscript, from the perspective of a publisher, and decide whether or not that manuscript is worthy of publication?

To make it easier find the answer, first consider some of the reasons for rejection.

Publishing is a business. As with any business, there is only so much money in the kitty, often dictated by the level of sales made during the previous year. Each book will cost a certain amount to produce. The amount of money in the kitty dictates the number of books that a publisher can afford to produce in any given period of time. A second element to this calculation is that a publisher employs X number of editors, compositors, proof-readers etc. X number of staff can do Y amount of work in any given period of time.

A rejection slip stating: *Sorry but our list is full,* means that the publisher has allocated all its available money, or staff, to the books it intends to publish during any given time period. In short, they do not possess the time, the money, or the staff to publish another title however worthy. Of course this is an over-simplification but it is a general principle.

Publishers also plan ahead, at least a year, often more. This planned list will include expected new books from their established authors along with commissioned books and special titles. Very often their list is full before some unexpected manuscript lands on their doormat. That manuscript is rejected, not because it's no good, but simply because, their list is full and will remain full for a good number of years ahead.

Another form of rejection involves a statement saying: Sorry, but this manuscript does not fit our list. The receipt of such a rejection illustrates a major fault on the part of the author submitting the manuscript. It should never have been submitted because that publisher does not publish that type or style of book. A major children's publisher I worked with would reject Thomas the Tank Engine, or Fireman Sam, or any story with similar characters because they do not publish stories with that style of character.

Another reason for rejection is simply that you are a new and unknown author. An established author will have a proven following, a readership that a good percentage of which can be guaranteed to purchase their next new title. The publisher is therefore guaranteed a certain level of sales, in return for a minimal level of promotion. And this is the crux of the matter.

Publishing is a business and the cost of publishing a book is an investment from which that publisher will expect a return. Achieving a satisfactory return, including a profit, is vital because this return dictates how many books that publisher can afford to publish in the next round. Publishing books that do not sell in a high enough volume to return a profit is a road to disaster. Therefore a perfectly good manuscript may well be rejected simply because the publisher does not believe that book will sell in a high enough volume to achieve their required return for the investment involved.

The level of investment required to promote a new title is increased dramatically by the need to promote any new and unknown author simply because promotion and advertising are expensive commodities. In many cases the first book by a new author will fail to make a profit, often-even fail to break even. But this is outweighed by the knowledge that the author has another book, and another in the pipeline, which will bring a future return.

Publishers are willing to gamble on new authors, but they do like to hedge their bets, which is why most new authors aren't totally new, but have previous publications under their belt. Look at the biographies of many authors and you will discover they have a previous career in journalism, writing for magazines, or some other claim to fame that aids their promotion as a new author. There is also the issue of, who you know. Don't gripe. That's life.

Publishing is a business and the purpose of any business is to sell the product it produces at a price higher than the cost of production. But this is where you have an advantage. Major publishers all have their big offices, their staff of editors, secretaries et al, all of which have to be paid for out of the income achieved by selling the books they produce. You do not, which means that your sales target, required to cover the cost of publication and achieve a profit, will be far lower than the sales target required by any major publisher. But you still have to do it the right way.

I am all in favour of author's publishing their own books and new technology makes this an increasingly viable proposition, but not self-publishing. Success depends on the author taking on the mantle, and hat, of becoming a publisher.

Within the publishing industry, the previous and sometimes still used term for such a publisher is, a *Small Press Publisher*. This has been modernised to the term, *Indie (Independent) Publisher*. An Indie publisher is a publisher that is not connected as an imprint name to any major publishing house and is one that commonly produces a small volume of books per year. Within the publishing industry, including the all important distribution and marketing side of this industry, a book published by an Indie or Small Press Publisher will be accepted and respected and accepted far easier than one that is termed as being self-published.

Ok, you can argue that there is no difference, but there is. An Indie Publisher, however small and even with only one title to their name, is a recognisable business entity. A mainstream publisher will look with licentious eyes at any book they believe will make them a profit and while they might reject getting involved in a struggle over the various rights issues that can arise when using one of the many, 'we will publish your book' companies, a book by an Indie publisher is a much easier target. They simply purchase the whole business, adding that imprint name to their raft of others. Consider the Octopus Publishing Group and its imprints: Conran Octopus - Bounty - Cassell illustrated - Gala Books - Godsfield Press - Hamlyn - Millers - Mitchell Beazley and Phillip's, all of which act as individual publishers and indeed, some were before becoming entwined in the all encompassing tentacles of the giant Octopus.

Of course this is a dream for the future, but do it properly and dreams can come true. The way to do it properly is not to self-publish, but to take off your author's hat and become a publisher, putting on a publisher's hat so that you approach the whole process, as would any other publisher. The next chapter will tell you how to take this first step.

BECOMING A PUBLISHER

You cannot publish your own book without first becoming a publisher and I will go so far as to say that there are many writers that believe they have self-published their own book but, because of this requirement, in truth they have done no such thing. Why this is so will be explained shortly.

The first step, as discussed in the previous chapter, is the need to approach the task from the perspective of a publisher, not as a writer. The next step is to become a real life, bona fide publisher. And doing this is easier than many might think.

There are two aspects to becoming a publisher. The first is that publishing is a business. The definition of a business is an entity or organisation that provides a service or produces a product with the intention to trade that product or service. Businesses come in different sizes ranging from the large multinational to the small sole trader, a common term for a one-person business. Most governments and especially the taxman will designate any individual that provides a service or produces a product for sale or reward as someone who is running a business, primarily because they want a cut of your profit. However, recognising this right at the beginning does have some benefits, which I will come to shortly.

This designation applies whether or not you have another job. Like many, you may have written your novel in your spare time, as a hobby, but now you're thinking about getting that book published and having collected the required number of rejection slips to push you towards publishing yourself, to hopefully sell more than just a few copies, you are starting a business. The taxman will view it this way and will also view you as being liable to pay tax on any income made from sales of the book you've just published. So you might as well do it right because doing it right can save a lot of hassle later on.

In many cases you don't need to do anything other than accept that what you are doing constitutes a small business. However, different countries have different laws and regulations so it is impossible to go into the exact details pertaining to every different situation. Even so, the principle rules are very similar.

You'll be likely be working at a computer, on a desk, in your own home so most business property regulations won't apply. Though there is a technicality that you might fall foul of when working from home. If a room in a house is used exclusively for business use, then certain taxes and regulations might apply. If that room is also used as a living room, dining room, bedroom, then they do not. Always check local regulations.

Another problem can come when the taxman

discovers you've been producing and selling books without declaring the income. This can apply even if you only sell 1 single copy, because the money from that sale counts as earned income unless, but I'll come to this.

The first step. As a business, you will require a business name. This can be any name you wish so long as it is not the same as any already established and registered business name. Once again, the laws and regulations relating to the regulation of business names vary from region to region and country to country, but in many cases you don't need to do anything other than choose a name.

In publishing, your business name will commonly correspond to the imprint name you will register as your publisher name, so if you to call your business, ABC Books, you would register your imprint name as, ABC Books. Another thing to consider when choosing a name is a little bit of snobbery that permeates certain regions of the publishing trade. There is, in some areas, an unwritten and often ignored convention of not using the words, 'books' or 'publishing' or 'Press' within your chosen imprint name. Therefore you have names like, Octopus, Harper Collins, Little Brown etc. Of course you can also come up with established publisher names that do include these words. As I said, it is an unwritten and often ignored convention that only a few purists might worry about.

Whatever name you choose, remember how

important it is to choose one that works and will continue to work well into the future because a name can be an important marketing tool or worse, a distraction. Consider the following lesson.

A married couple decided to open a cafe. His name was Sam and her name was Ella and they thought, what better than call it Sam and Ella's, after all, they were aiming for that comfortable homey feel about their cafe. The only problem is that spoken allowed, Sam & Ella's sounds too much like Salmonella, a rather nasty stomach bug caused by eating bad food. Remember the law of unexpected consequences!

To become a publisher you need to register your imprint name with the relevant ISBN Agency for whatever country you're in. Each individual publisher is identified by the ISBN (International Standard Book Number) they are assigned. You cannot be a publisher unless you have an ISBN number assigned to your name.

This brings us back to the point about those that believe they have self-published their own book, doing so by paying one of the many companies that advertises such a service. However, in doing so, many of these companies also provide the ISBN number under which that book is registered.

Consider the breakdown of the International Book Numbering System:

The first 3 numbers are the Prefix element, always 3 digits in length and currently either 978 or 979.

The comes the Registration group element that identifies the particular country, geographic region or language group participating in the ISBN system.

The Registrations element identifies the particular publisher within that group, the imprint name under which any book is registered.

The Publication element, the next 3 numbers identifies the individual book belonging to that publisher.

The final number is a check digit because the ISBN, as a whole calculates to a specific equation meaning any error is immediately flagged for correction.

Therefore, if any book production service provides the ISBN number for your book and that number is one purchased and registered under their name, then they are the registered publisher. They can call it self-publishing and any author that has used such a service to publish their book can believe they have self-published until the cows come home, but the truth is, they haven't. The registration element part of the ISBN number identifies the publisher and unless this is an ISBN number purchased by you from the relevant ISBN Agency and registered under imprint name of your own choosing, then you haven't published your own book.

To purchase an ISBN number or block of numbers,

always more efficient, contact the relevant ISBN Agency for the country in which you live.

The ISBN Agency in the U.K is Nielsen. In America it is Bowker. A simply search on-line will lead to the relevant agency website and this will provide all the information you need to register and purchase your first block of ISBN numbers, probably your first genuine business expense.

Which brings us back to the nature of business and the taxman. In becoming a publisher and setting out to publish your first book, you will incur a number of expenses before getting to the stage of actually offering that book for sale.

Consider one of the examples given in the chapter on the Vanity Trap. Someone pays £1,000 to have a book published. They sell 100 copies, giving them a return of £559.20 and although this is a loss, the taxman will view that £559.20 as earned income and demand a share. But if they've done things properly and kept records, as everyone should, this legitimate business expense of whatever amount it is can be put against that income.

Technically and depending on relevant tax regulations, this loss of £440.80 can be carried forward and counted against the following years income. All legitimate business expenses, including paper, printer ink, postage, and even depreciation on equipment can be counted against tax. All that is needed is to keep the relevant records and receipts. You might even be allowed to charge these costs against income from any other employment you may have.

All of a sudden becoming a publisher and starting a business doesn't seem so bad. However, I am not an accountant. I have a son married to one, but tax regulations vary from country to country and you shouldn't need an accountant at this stage. But if you do, their fees are also deductible as a legitimate business expense. What you must do is keep records of every expense because you'll need them when you start selling your books.

And now for another little tax anomaly that only applies in some European countries.

VAT (Value Added Tax) is a tax on sales that everyone pays whenever they purchase an item that is subject to VAT. This anomaly arises because not ever product or service is subject to VAT. In truth they are but some products and services are, for VAT purposes, viewed as zero-rated.

For the ordinary person on the street, VAT is part of the purchase price; you pay it and think no more. It is a different matter for a business that is registered for VAT. It is a legal requirement for any business with a turnover that exceeds £85,000 in any twelve-month period to register for VAT. Note that this is turnover, not profit and the twelve-month period does not need to correspond to the tax or calendar year. A business also needs to register if they exceed the relevant percentage turnover in any 30 day period, but for most small businesses, none of this will apply. However, any business, even one with a turnover far below the level that makes it necessary, can voluntarily register for VAT.

The question is, why would any business voluntarily register for the rigours of the VAT tax system?

The answer is, whether you are registered or not, you will pay VAT on any equipment you purchase, all consumables you use and of course, printing and distribution etc. The VAT you pay on these products, services etc, is called your Input Tax. The VAT you charge on the products you sell is called your Output Tax. The main idea of business is to sell the product or service you provide for more that the cost of the raw materials, consumables and any equipment you purchase. Therefore the Output Tax will always be higher than the Input Tax and in the VAT calculation, the Input Tax is deducted from the Output Tax and that business only pays the difference in the two totals.

This is where it becomes interesting.

Even a small publisher can run up a large total of Input VAT, but books are one of those items that, for VAT purposes, are zero-rated. Therefore a publisher will pay out VAT on everything from sundry items to the cost of book production, yet take in absolutely no VAT from the sale of the books they produce. Note this only applies to physical books, not e-books etc. The result is that at the end of any VAT accounting period, the publisher receives a huge cheque for repayment of the VAT they've paid out during that period.

A regular cheque from the tax office, what more could anyone ask for. But of course there is a drawback. Compared to a VAT Inspector, an ordinary tax inspector is all sweetness and light. There is no allowance for error or inaccuracy and large penalties if any do occur. Also, like the Mafia, once in it is hard to get out. Plus, the cost of employing a VAT qualified accountant may outweigh any benefit.

Note that this section is included as information only and I do not recommend you do this, but if tempted, do not do anything without discussing the issue with a qualified accountant and relevant VAT authority and on your head be it.

KNOWING THE MARKET

Now we move on to the practical side of bringing a book to publication and you are wondering why I'm starting with the market instead of editing or something related to the physical aspects of book production. I am starting here because the purpose of publishing a book is to bring that book to the market. To do that you need to choose the format and the size of the print run and before you can make those decisions, you need to know the potential size of the market and how to access that market.

I was also torn as to whether to put this chapter before the previous one, on becoming a publisher. The question being, do you even need to become a publisher before you are sure there is a market for the book you intend to publish?

On this question, I need to accept the basics, that your manuscript is well written and contains everything needed to make it worthy of publication, even when looking at it through the cold, calculating eye of a publisher.

Bringing a book to market creates questions that go beyond the literary merit of the story and the quality of the writing. The answers to these questions dictate the format and style of the finished book, along with the size of the initial print run and how the book will be presented to the market. Another very important aspect will be the planned price point of the finished book and in this, virtually every self-publisher makes the mistake of focussing on getting their book published, in the belief that every aspect of the market will fall into place when they get to the point of trying to sell that book. It doesn't and it never will.

The price/cost conundrum

There are two methods used for setting the price of any product. The price of some products is sold at a wholesale price with the retailer given a suggested 'mark up' to achieve that product's retail price. Other products are given a set retail price and then the retailer is given a discount on this price. The percentages in both the mark-up and discount processes can be varied according to quantity or other factors, which is where negotiation between buyer and seller come into play. A good salesperson will know the boundaries in which to operate, as will the buyer. As a small independent small press publisher, you will be responsible for selling your own book, so you need to know how. We'll come to that, but this is the starting point.

Books are commonly sold using the discount process. For example, lets say that the retail price of your book is going to be £9.99. The standard discount expected in any bookshop is 35%. Of course the price of finished books will vary, depending on size, format etc., but a standard discount of 35% is about normal. This can rise to 50%, sometimes more depending on the quantity ordered and other factors. As an agent, I've walked into distributors and large chains where the starting point has been a 50% discount on retail before they'll even talk. Of course we're talking about volume and orders running into four figure values. Then, operating as a small Indie publisher on my own account, I sold 98 copies of a new title within the first week. Both facts make any vanity publisher's claim that selling 100 books equals a bestseller look totally laughable.

However, this detracts from the point. The retail price for your book is set by what the market will accept, not by the cost of publication plus whatever you want as profit. Therefore, do your market research and take a stroll around any bookstore, scroll through online stores as well. Most books fall into specific price brackets, case bound (hard back) books being more expensive than paperbacks. Most publishers release a new title as a case bound book first because, although these sell in fewer quantity, they produce a higher per book profit than the mass-produced paperback that will inevitably follow.

So lets assume that the word count of the manuscript you intend to publish will produce a case bound book with a page count comparable to other similar titles. These books commonly retail around the £17.99 mark. You have to be able to give at least 35% discount. So that's £17.99 - £6.29 = £11.70. Give a discount of 50% and that's £17.99 - £8.99 = £8.99. Therefore you have to produce your book at a per book cost of less than £8.99 to achieve a profit.

Do this same calculation for a paperback book and you're looking at a maximum allowable per book production cost of around £3 or £4.

But the cost of publishing a book is not just the cost of production. As previously mentioned, a publisher has to cover the cost of all their overheads, delivery, staff wages and other expenses. This is where the small, independent, especially the sole trader publisher as the advantage. Your overheads will be much less than an established publisher but the calculation still applies. Each book published and produced must bear a percentage of the total cost of production, the individual per book cost plus a percentage of overheads. So the larger the print run the wider this overhead cost is spread. Production costs are also reduced by increasing the volume of the print run.

Now you might think this is all very academic, but it is the key difference between business success and business failure. Any business must be able to produce and market their product at a cost lower than the price at which that product will be sold. Remember that unless you're going to rely totally on direct sales, you will need to allow that any retail outlet or distributor will all want their cut. And as stated above, this retail price is dictated by what the market will accept, not the other way round. The rule is:

THE RETAIL PRICE OF A BOOK IS SET BY WHAT THE MARKET WILL ACCEPT.
THEREFORE THE ALLOWABLE COST OF PRODUCTION IS ALSO SET BY WHAT THE MARKET WILL ACCEPT.

To put a number on this, divide the retail price of your book by 10 and you have the, per book, printing cost that most established publishers will aim for. Of course, as a small independent publisher, you can allow a little lee way, but as a target, try to keep your per book printing cost below 30% of the cover price.

This is one of the first calculations made by all mainstream publishers, often leading to a rejection slip simply because the math does not point to a potential profit. In mainstream publishing, the profit margin can be as tight as only 1 or 2 pence per book, but a few hundred thousand pennies are still worth having. Less and you see how tight it becomes.

You do not go ahead and produce your book at whatever cost is quoted and then set the retail price needed to recoup that cost, as do many self-publishers. You restrain production costs within the confines of what the market will accept, by any means possible or, as a publisher, be willing to accept that the project is not viable. Can you do that, as a writer who has laboured away over many years to produce a book? This is what is meant by wearing a publisher's hat.

However, you will be pleased to hear that this is not the end of the story. As an Indie Publisher, you won't have those overheads. As this is your own title, what would be paid in author royalties goes into the same pot. Plus, you can accept a loss on your first book, in your first year, because there will be a second book and a third, with each title building on the success of the first.

Consider also the simple fact that very few small businesses make a profit in their first year and very few publishers make a profit on the first edition of a new book by a new author. Building a market for a new author is a long term process and as a new publisher, you are also entering a crowded market, more so because new technology means everyone can do it. This makes is more important to do it properly and plan the process, not only as an author, but also as a publisher.

Now consider these comparisons. To produce 1,000 copies of a 500 page 8"x 5" trade paperback, a certain print production service quoted a price that works out at £4.50 per copy. A standard retail-selling price of a book in this size and format is about £6.99. Remember that most bookshops will want at least 35% discount on the selling price, distributors 50% or more. This means your trade-selling price is will likely be less than your production cost, and this is without considering any overheads.

However, the same production service quoted a production cost for 1,000 6"x 9" case bound books that calculates to £7.25 per copy. The retail-selling price of a book of this format can be around the £20.00 mark. Give a trade discount of 50% and there is still room to play with. Consider also that within a few minutes of scouting production costs on the Internet, I discovered another company that quoted a price that worked out to £6.73 per copy and I know this cost can be trimmed even further.

Remember that, as a publisher, you will be looking for a book production service, in short, a printer, because most printers have the ability to produce books at a price and quality that is acceptable to the market. This rules out any company that advertises that they will *self-publish* your book for you. Surely that is a contradiction in terms!

The rule is that the larger the print run, the lower the per book cost. Of course this requires an upfront investment in printing your book, but at least this way you will have books to sell. And there is the rule that you can't sell a book unless you have a book to sell, or at least, it's a lot easier to sell a book in the hand than one that has yet to be printed.

But of course, this huge up front cost may be a big stumbling block, which brings us to the choice of format for your book.

Book Format

If we're talking about publishing a physical book, the choice is between case bound, (hard cover) and paperback (soft cover). While there is a wide variety in book sizes there are also several standard sizes to aim for. A mass-market paperback will be 4¼"x 7". A trade paperback can be 5½"x 8½". Case bound books tend to be larger, 6"x9" or 6¼"x9½". These are just a few examples and you can choose any size you wish, though keeping to one of the market standard sizes is obviously the best choice. Bookshop shelving, as with standard bookshelves for home use, is designed to take books of a standard size. A bookshop buyer can reject a book simply because it won't fit the shelf size in their shop. More detail on book formats is provided in a subsequent chapter.

Print On Demand, or short run publishing is just another method of producing a physical book. The only real alternative is an e-book and there are several e-book providers, such as Amazon Kindle, where you can incur no up-front cost for publication. The same applies to Amazon's Create Space POD service and others, such as Blurb, Bookbaby, Lulu, etc. With the availability of virtually no cost e-book and POD services, it is a wonder some people still pay hundreds if not thousands to some *'we will publish your book'* company. But publishing a book is the easy part. Selling that book is where things become difficult.

When it comes to e-books, you need to understand that this is a different market from the physical book market. As a generalisation, the younger generation will opt for an e-book version while the older generation prefer to feel a book in their hand rather than on some electronic device. In addition, although there was an initial switch to e-readers when they were first introduced, a growing number of people, including younger readers, are switching back to real books. Many use both, an e-reader for convenience, a real book whenever they can. If you publish solely as an e-book, you could be missing out on a whole section of the market. Most publishers use both. First comes the case bound edition, sales less than a paperback but a larger per book profit. Followed by a paperback edition and then an e-book edition.

Now, before sitting down to publish, you need to know the market potential for your book. Knowing the market allows you to decide in which format to publish, the print run and, which manuscript to publish.

Choosing the Manuscript to Publish

There are millions of books out there and thousands more are published every year. A Bowker report, for the USA, reveals, in 2015, there was a release of over 300,000 books from mainstream publishers with an additional 700,000 being self-published. In addition, another 13 million previously published books are still in print and available to the market. The number of books available has increased dramatically at the same time as, the same report reveals, bookstore sales are down by 37% and that even if you do everything right, your book only a 1% chance of being stocked by a bookstore.

Things aren't much better in the e-book market. The introduction of e-readers sparked a dramatic surge in e-book sales, which flattened off in 2013 and has now fallen by more than 10% and it is getting harder and harder each year to find a market for any new book published. But if you're reading this, I will assume that you are determined to go ahead; so it is even more important that the book you choose to publish has a distinctive USP.

The term USP stands for, Unique Selling Point. It is a term marketing and sales people bandy about and apply to every product made. What is its USP? Why should anyone buy this one instead of buying some other brand? So what is your book's USP? For example: If your book is a crime novel, what makes is different from any other crime novel out there? Apply this question whatever the genre.

There is also the simple fact that non-fiction is easier to market than fiction. With non-fiction, it is easier to argue that the book looks at any given subject from a unique perspective, or reveals a new discovery, or fits a particular niche section of the market. There will also be a definable group of readers that are interested in that subject, whatever it is. Previous sales records help any publisher define the size of this interest and therefore the potential size of the market. Of course you are unlikely to have access to such information but other forms of market research can still help define the potential market for any given title. Knowing how many books will sell will help you choose the most cost effective print run for their production.

Fiction, in any genre, is just fiction, a made up story dependent on plot and character and the author's imagination for its success. So what has your imagination brought to an already saturated market that makes your story different? What is its USP? Once you can answer this you can start to plan your marketing strategy, which is something mainstream publishers do before they decide to go ahead and publish. If you're going to do this properly, you need to do the same. Now comes the hard part.

If your reading this, you've already decided to publish

and you've already decided on which manuscript you want to see in print, from the perspective of a writer. Now you need to step back and judge the situation as a publisher and as hard as this may seem, are you able to reject the manuscript you'd planned to publish in favour of another?

You may only have the one, but as a writer, you may also have more than one manuscript, either finished, part finished or in need to work. This may involve a delay, but a person should never rush into loosing money, or wasting time and effort on a project that is going to be pitched into an overcrowded and declining market. To stand any chance of success, you need to get it right. You also need to know the hurdles you will face, not some puerile guide to self-publishing that makes it seem easy.

If you are ready and determined to go ahead, now we'll begin.

PUBLISHING CONTRACTS & RIGHTS

So you're going to publish your own book, so you don't need a contract. Or so you think!

First there is you, the author. Then there is you, the publisher. Then there is the potential that your book may well be a success, though limited by the fact that you are a small independent publisher without the market clout of a well-established publishing house. One of these may see that success, after all, it is their business to study the market and watch for anything new. They may see your success and wish to pick up your novel, or even take over your imprint name. Established publishers are used to contracts. They expect a contract to exist. They understand them. Having a contract makes you appear more professional. Having a contract defines the rights that are available, or signed away, plus, having a contract is just standard process. This stands despite the fact any contract can be torn up with the agreement of both parties which, when both parties are the same person, makes the process appear irrelevant.

However, it's your decision. What follows are some of the key elements that should be found in a publishing contract, a sample contract along with some elements to avoid.

Another question, before going further. One covered all ready but really, really important, If you use a self-publishing service, why should you, as some insist, need to sign a publishing contract? If they want you to sign a contract, it should be a contract for book production and nothing more, with no mention of rights or any such issue.

So what should you expect to be in a publishing contract? What follows is the layout of an average contract and what these clauses mean.

(1) A statement of what is being licensed to the publisher. This could be First Serial Rights, All Rights, or a list of specific rights. This statement is usually entitled: Licence of Grant.

(2) A statement of countries in which this licence or grant applies. For example, this could be just Great Britain, or just America, or Europe, or Worldwide, stating where the publisher has the right to sell or sub-license the book.

(3) A statement of advances, if any, may be paid, in a single payment, or half on signature, half on publication, or in thirds, or even in quarters, though this is more common where the advance is substantial.
Note that an Advance is what it says. It is an advance in

royalties against expected sales, not in addition to royalties on those sales. In theory, if sales do not reach the expected level, the publisher can reclaim any advance paid, though they rarely do.

(4) A statement on the level of royalties to be paid and when. This can be yearly, bi-annually or quarterly. Royalties can be paid on either the retail or wholesale price of the book. The level of royalties can also be staged, depending on the level of sales, rising as sales increase. For example: The royalty level may start at a base royalty of 10% on hardbacks, 7.5% on paperbacks, 5% on board or novelty books with this level increasing at sales achieve certain stated levels. *(Note: All royalty amounts are subject to negotiation).*

(5) A statement of Subsidiary rights. These include reprint rights, large print editions, book club editions, paperback reprint, etc., serial rights (the right to publish in newspapers and magazines), anthology and quotation rights, educational rights, audio rights, e-book rights and so on. The percentage royalty to be paid should be listed against each right. Rights listed in the sub-rights clause should be checked against the opening grant of rights clause to confirm that they conform.

(6) A statement of delivery and publication. This is a

clause, or clauses, that state the agreed delivery date of the book along with an undertaking by the publisher to publish the work within a stated period of time.

(7) Copyright and moral rights. As an author you are licensing the publication of your work, so you should retain copyright and this clause should oblige the publisher to include a copyright line in every edition of the work however published or sub-licensed by them. The author's moral rights are also often asserted within the contract.

(8) Publishers generally insist on having the final say regarding details of production, publication and advertising, though they should also consult with the author over the blurb, catalogue copy, jacket and cover design. This clause should include an undertaking to supply the author with a proof copy, giving the author enough time to check the proof copy for any error that may have occurred during the book design process.

(9) The contract should state the dates on which author sales accounts will be published, including the dates that royalties will be paid for each sales accounting period. This is usually twice a year, however. The layout and detail including in royalty statements vary from publisher to publisher and mistakes are more common than one might imagine. The author should check these

statements and immediately raise any anomalies with the publisher.

(10) Like any business, publishers can go bust and some fail to stick to the agreed terms of a contract. The contract should include a 'reversion' clause stating that in such circumstances, the author shall regain all the rights covered within the contract. This clause should also contain a segment stating that if the publisher allows the book to go out of print, the publisher may only hold onto the rights covered in the contract for a stated period of time. If this period is exceeded, the author regains the rights involved.

(11) The contract should include a statement saying that the publisher cannot assign any of the rights granted to them by the author without the author's express written consent. For example, if a small publishing company is taken over by a larger publishing house, the original publisher cannot assign any rights to the larger company without the author's consent.

What follows is a sample contract with all the various clauses, repeating much of what was stated before but written as an actual contract could be worded.

* * *

CONTRACT

This contract is between ....
Hereinafter called: the author

And

....
Hereinafter called: the Publisher

1. GRANT

The author hereby grants and assigns to the Publisher the exclusive rights to publish in the English language in book form in all countries of the world, a Work now entitled <<Title of book>> (hereinafter called the Work), which title may be changed only by mutual consent in writing.

2. REPRESENTATIONS AND WARRANTIES

The Author represents that he is the sole proprietor of the Work and that the Work to the best of his knowledge does not contain any libellous matter and does not violate the civil rights of any person or persons, does not infringe any existing copyright and has not heretofore been published in book form. The Author shall hold harmless and indemnify the publisher from any recovery finally sustained by reason of any violations of copyright or other property of personal right; provided, however, that the Publisher shall with all reasonable promptness notify the Author of any claim or suit which may involve the warranties of the Author hereunder; and the Author agrees fully to cooperate in the defence thereof. The warranties contained in this article do not extend to drawings, illustrations, insofar as not furnished by the Author, or to any other material not furnished by the Author.

3. DELIVERY

The Author agrees to deliver to the publisher, a complete typewritten script as well as a complete electronic text of the Work in a format to be determined by the Publisher (hereinafter called the Script). If the Script shall not have been delivered within three (3) months after the date this agreement is signed the Publisher may, at its option, terminate this agreement by notice in writing posted or delivered to the Author.

4. PUBLICATION

The Publisher agrees to publish the Work in book form at its own expense at a catalogue retail price of not less than $60 per copy not later than twelve months after the delivery of the completed Work. In the event of delay from causes beyond the control of the Publisher, the publication date may be postponed accordingly, but not to exceed eighteen months from the delivery of the completed work.

5. COPYRIGHT

The Publisher, upon first publication of the

Work, agrees duly to copyright it with the relevant authority in the Netherlands in the name of the Author, and to take all necessary steps to protect the copyright under the Universal Copyright Convention. The Author shall, upon the termination of the first term, make timely application for renewal of copyright under then existing copyright law and, provided this agreement shall then be in force and effect, the Author agrees to assign to the Publisher, for the renewal term of the copyright, the rights herein granted to the Publisher.

6. EDITING AND PROOFREADING

The Publisher shall make no changes in, additions to, or eliminations from the manuscript without the consent of the Author, and in order to obtain such consent, shall submit the copy-edited manuscript to the Author for his approval. The Author agrees to return such proof to the Publisher with his corrections within thirty (30) days of the receipt thereof by him. The cost of alterations required by the Author, other than corrections of typesetting errors, in excess of fifteen percent (15%) of the original cost of composition, shall be charged against the earnings of the Author under this agreement or shall, at the option of the Publisher, be paid by the Author in cash; provided, however, that the Publisher shall upon request promptly furnish to the Author an itemized statement of such additional expenses, and shall make available at the Publisher's office the corrected proof for inspection by the Author or his representatives.

7. ROYALTIES AND LICENSES

The Publisher shall pay to the Author or his duly authorised representatives, the following advances and royalties:

(a) A royalty of ten percent (10%) of the retail price thereof on all copies of the Work sold less returns.

(b) Fifty percent (50%) of the proceeds of any license granted to another Publisher to bring out a reprint edition of the Work.

(c) No royalties shall be payable of copies furnished to the Author or on copies for review, sample, or other similar purposes, or on copies destroyed.

The Author or his duly authorised representatives shall have the right upon written request to examine the books of account of the Publisher insofar as they relate to the Work and any other of the Author's works under contract to the Publisher. Such examination shall be at the cost of the Author unless errors of accounting amounting to five percent (5%) or more of the total sum paid to the Author shall be found to his disadvantage, in which case the cost shall be borne by the Publisher.

8. OVERPAYMENT

In all instances in which the Author shall have received an overpayment of monies under the terms hereof, the Publisher may deduct such overpayment from any further sums payable to the Author in respect to the Work.

9. NOTIFICATIONS AND PAYMENT

The Publisher agrees promptly to advise the Author of the terms of any contracts entered into for any grant or license permitted under this agreement whenever the Author's share of the proceeds or royalty is one hundred dollars ($100.00) or more. The Publisher shall make such contracts available to the Author or his representative at the office of the Publisher, and a copy thereof will be furnished the Author upon his written request. The Publisher shall promptly pay the Author's share of such proceeds or royalty to him upon receipt.

10. AUTHOR'S COPIES

The Author shall be permitted to purchase copies for his personal use at a discount of forty percent (XX%) of the retail price.

11. STATEMENTS AND PAYMENTS

The Publisher agrees to render semi-annual statements on July 31 and January 31 (or other stated date) in each year following the publication hereof, showing an account of sales and all other payments due hereunder to June 31 and December 31 (or other stated date) preceding said respective accounting dates. Payment then due shall accompany such statements.

12. REVERSION AND TERMINATION

(a) At any time after two years from the date of first publication, but not before, the Publisher may on three months' notice in writing to the Author or his representative discontinue publication, and in that event this agreement shall terminate and all rights hereunder shall revert to the Author at the expiration of said (to be negotiated) period.

(b) If the Publisher shall, during the existence of this agreement, default in the delivery of semi-annual statements or in the making of payments as herein provided and shall neglect or refuse to deliver such statements or make such payments, or any of them, within thirty (30) days after written notice of such default, this agreement shall terminate at the expiration of such thirty (30) days without prejudice to the Author's claim for any monies which may have accrued under this agreement or to any other rights and remedies to which the Author may be entitled.

(c) If the Publisher shall fail to publish the Work within the period in Paragraph 4 provided, or otherwise fail to comply with or fulfil the terms and conditions hereof, or in the event of

bankruptcy, etc., as in Paragraph 13 hereof
provided, this agreement shall terminate and the
rights herein granted to the Publisher shall revert
to the Author. In such event all payments
theretofore made to the Author shall belong to the
Author without prejudice to any other remedies that
the Author may have.

(d) Upon the termination of this agreement for
any cause under this Article or Article 13 hereof,
all rights granted to the Publisher shall revert
to the Author for his use at any time and the
Publisher shall return to the Author all property
originally furnished by the Author.

13. BANKRUPTCY AND INSOLVENCY

If a petition in bankruptcy shall be filed by or
against the Publisher, or if it shall be adjudged
insolvent by any court, or if a Trustee or a
Receiver of any property of the Publisher shall be
appointed in any suit or proceeding by or against
the Publisher, or if the Publisher shall make an
assignment for the benefit of creditors or shall
take the benefit of any bankruptcy or insolvency
Act, or if the Publisher shall liquidate its
business for any cause whatsoever, this agreement
shall terminate automatically without notice, and
such termination shall be effective as of date of
the filing of such petition, adjudication,
appointment, assignment or declaration or
commencement of reorganisation or liquidation

proceedings, and all rights granted hereunder shall thereupon revert to the Author.

14. RESERVED RIGHTS

All rights in the Work now existing, or which may hereafter come into existence, not specifically herein granted are reserved to the Author for his use at any time. Reserved publication rights include, but are not limited to, the right to publish or cause to be published in any form, excerpts, summaries of the Work, thereof, not to exceed seventy-five hundred (7,500) words in length.

15. ASSIGNMENT

No assignment of this contract, voluntary or by operation of law, shall be binding upon either of the parties without the written consent of the other; provided, however, that the Author may assign or transfer any monies due or to become due under this agreement.

16. ARBITRATION

Any controversy or claim arising out of this agreement or the breach thereof shall be settled by arbitration in accordance with the rules then obtaining. Such arbitration shall be held in the City of Leiden unless otherwise agreed by the parties. The Author may, at his option, in the case of failure to pay royalties, refuse to arbitrate, and pursue his legal remedies.

17. NOTICES

Any written notice required under any of the
provisions of this agreement shall be deemed to
have been properly served by delivery in person or
by mailing the same in paper or by electronic means
to the parties hereto at the addresses set forth
above, except as the addresses may be changed by
notice in writing; provided, however, that notices
of termination shall be sent by registered mail.

18. WAIVER

A waiver of any breach of this agreement or of
any of the terms or conditions by either party
thereto, shall not be deemed a waiver of any
repetition of such breach or in any wise affect any
other terms or conditions hereof; no waiver shall
be valid or binding unless it shall be in writing,
and signed by the parties.

19. INFRINGEMENT

If during the existence of this agreement the
copyright shall be infringed, the Publisher may,
at its own cost and expense, take such legal action,
in the Author's name if necessary, as may be
required to restrain such infringement or to seek
damages therefor. The Publisher shall not be liable
to the Author for the Publisher's failure to take
such legal steps. If the Publisher does not bring
such an action, the Author may do so in his name

at his own cost and expense. Money damages recovered for an infringement shall be applied first toward the repayment of the expense of bringing and maintaining the action, and thereafter the balance shall belong to the Author, provided, however, that any money damages recovered on account of a loss of the Publisher's profits shall be divided equally between the Author and the Publisher.

20. DOCUMENTS

If any of the rights granted to the Publisher revert to the Author, the Publisher shall execute all documents, which may be necessary or appropriate to revert all such rights in the Author.

21. LAW

This agreement shall be construed in accordance with the laws of the (relevant country).

22. INHERITANCE

This agreement shall be binding upon and inure to the benefit of the heirs, executors, administrators and assigns of the Author, and upon and to the successors and assigns of the Publisher.

23. ALTERATION

This agreement may not be modified, altered or changed except by an instrument in writing signed by the Author and the Publisher.

    24. APPROVAL
    Notwithstanding anything to the contrary herein
contained, the Publisher shall obtain the Author's
written advance approval of any jacket or cover
design, including the text thereof, to be used in
connection with the Work, and of any contracts with
third parties for the publication of the Work;
which approval shall not be unreasonably withheld.

The contract would then be signed by the author and by the publisher along with witness signatures, one witness for the author, one for the publisher.

And now some contract clauses to avoid.

Apart from the previously mentioned pulping clause, there are clauses, or clause elements, that should not be in the contract and if they are, this is a contract you should not agree to sign. Such clauses are an aberration to all genuine publishers.

(1) Advance too low or paid in too slow stages.

An advance is based on an author's credentials as a writer and calculated on anticipated sales. The only variation to this is with new authors where no such calculation can be made so if offered a contract, any advance may well be very low or even non-existent, especially if the publisher is a small independent.

(2) The royalty rate is too low.

Royalties can be calculated either on the net, wholesale, or gross, retail list price of a book. As stated previously, there should be an escalating scale depending on sales called royalty breaks. For example, a publisher might state a royalty rate of 10% for the first 10,000 sales, 12% for the next 10,000, rising to 14% or15% thereafter. The higher the sales the greater the % royalties. Be wary if this escalating scale segment is missing from the contract. Note that the 40%, 60%, even 80% royalty figure quoted by some self-publishing service providers is meaningless because 80% of nothing is still less than 10% of something.

(3) Related to the above. A sub-clause stating that book club and other subsidiary sales do not count, or count at a very low percentage, towards royalties or when calculating royalty breaks.

(4) A deep discount clause.

The royalty rate is slashed on books sold at a discount on the publisher's stated retail price. Considering that, as a marketing tool, many books are sold at a discount, this can dig deeply into the royalties an author should receive. While this can increase sales, thus increasing potential royalties, the author needs to keep any discount percentage on their royalties to a minimum.

(5) A strict reserve against return clause.

Publishers are entitle to withhold a percentage of royalties against returns of unsold books from bookstores, but this percentage should be fair and reasonable.

(6) Skewed or unclear distribution of subsidiary rights.

These include magazine articles, book clubs, film, audiotapes, foreign sales and electronic rights.

(7) A vague out of print clause, as mentioned near the start of this chapter.

(8) Copyright in the publisher's name, either in the contract or front matter of the book. Copyright should always be in the author's name.

(9) Draconian penalties for late delivery of the manuscript.

(10) A strict option clause.

An option clause gives the publisher first option on the author's next manuscript. Such a clause needs to include a response time; the maximum time the publisher has to say yes or no. Delaying this decision prevents the author seeking another publisher until it is made.

(11) A non-competition clause that prevents the author writing another book on a similar subject for submission to another publisher.

(12) A clause requiring the author to repay the publisher any advance made prior to publication if the

publisher then decides to cancel publication.

Despite being rarely used, publishers have the right to reclaim any advances paid if sales to not achieve the required level, but if the publisher decides to cancel publication, the responsibility for this loss lies with the publisher, not the author.

(13)

Missing clauses that should be in the contract.

These include an audit clause, a clause giving the author the right to audit the publisher's sales accounts.

A bankruptcy clause. Any business can go bankrupt and all assets of that business get seized by the official receiver, or similar depending on which country you are in. This will include the rights to your manuscript, unless protected by a specific clause stating that in such a circumstance, all rights revert to the author.

Any of the other clauses or clause elements outlined in the first part of this chapter.

THE PUBLISHING PROCESS

Now we can move on to the actual business of publishing and book production.

The publishing process is a series of steps and as publisher you have a choice concerning each one of these steps. Each will be expanded on as we proceed giving the criteria by which you can make that choice when it arises.

Step 1. Choosing the manuscript to publish.

But you're reading this because you intend to publish your own book so the answer is obvious. But is it? I know I'm repeating myself but this is an important decision. This is and should always be a marketing decision. If you've written more than one manuscript, even if one of the others needs more work, which one of these manuscripts has the greatest market potential?

Step 2. Story Editing.

This is to ensure that the basic requirements of the story are correct. These elements include the plot, asking the question whether the plot works, or not, characterisation, asking whether the characters maintain their assigned character and appear real, or not. Then there are questions surround any sub-plot and general construction. Does the story flow? Do elements take place in a logical sequence and continue until they arrive at a satisfactory conclusion? A story must reach a satisfactory conclusion without leaving elements hanging. Never leave the reader asking, what happened to...? Unless of course there is a planned sequel.

Story editing raises questions that the author cannot answer because the story is in the author's head and they know what they mean even if the reader doesn't. This is why, if the author insists on self-editing, the suggestion is to leave the manuscript sitting on a shelf for at least six months before attempting to story edit.

Step 3. Copy-Editing.

Copy-editing, also called line-editing or sub-editing, often leading to the mistaken belief that this is somewhat less than story editing. Copy-editing is not concerned with the story in the same way as a story editor, instead it involves an examination and correction of the grammatical construction used by the writer while avoiding any alteration to what might be called, the individual author's style.

Step 4. Book Design and Layout.

This involves setting out the page design of your book,

front matter, body text and back matter. There are a few basic principles to follow but it is not too difficult a task once these principles are explained.

At one time this setting out or design process led to the preparation of camera-ready artwork, done using a mechanical or paste-up system to create a negative ready for offset litho printing. Book layout and design is now mostly done using digital desktop-publishing (DTP) software resulting in the output of a PDF (Portable Document Format) file. This PDF file is then used to prepare all subsequent print preparation work for whichever print method is to be used. A book will commonly require the preparation of two PDF files; one PDF file for the cover and one PDF file for the page content.

Book layout and design is largely an artistic process, the designer concentrating on the *look* of each page, along with a series of layout rules that will be described further on. That said, it is not too difficult to undertake this task yourself.

You will need a suitable DTP application and by suitable I mean, the main requirement is the ability to output the PDF file format.

While some DTP applications, such as Quark and Adobe In Design are quite (very) expensive to purchase, there are a number of sub £100/$100 applications that will do the job just as well. Major applications such as In Design will do far more than is required for the basic print layout required when setting out a standard book and can achieve a similar quality result.

E-book publishing has different requirements. Different e-book suppliers require your manuscript file to be in a specific file format, such as Word. They then require that you apply specific elements to the text format and text layout of your manuscript file before uploading. Most supply templates and full directions to enable you to do this yourself.

Step 5. Book Production.

Book production consists of two main parts. The first is printing.

The publisher's task is to choose the method of book production most viable for the style of book they wish to produce. If this is to be an e-book then the publisher should compare the benefits and drawbacks of each e-book service provider. If it is to be a physical book the same comparison needs to be made. Those companies that advertise a publishing service for a fee should be viewed as book production companies and nothing more, comparing the service they provide with that of any book printer. You might be surprised to learn that virtually any local printer can produce books at a far lower cost than many of the companies that advertise a book self-publishing service.

Print finishing is a separate task from the task of printing and there are companies that specialise in print finishing work. In times gone by such a company would be called a Bindery, where books are bound. Printing and print finishing are commonly combined but are still two separate parts of the book production process.

Depending on the printing process, print finishing includes the separate processes of folding, collating, binding and trimming, each involving its own separate cost. I say that because the more you can do yourself, the more you reduce your per book cost. The more you reduce your per book cost, the more viable the end price of your book becomes when introduced to the market. As we proceed, I will show you how you can undertake each and every one of these production tasks, from lay out and design, to printing, to binding and trimming. In short, I will explain how to set up your own Print On Demand process, and it's not as difficult as it sounds.

Step 6. Proof Reading.

This is a final page check of a proof print version of your book. By this stage the textual content should be correct. Any changes and corrections required should have been picked up during the editing process, but sometimes you'll come across computer generated layout glitches that need correcting. Any changes now can alter the whole text flow of the document so after correcting your proof copy, print another and check that.

Your task, as a publisher, is to produce a finished book of suitable quality at a marketable retail price. Achieving a marketable retail price requires strict control over each element of cost. Each of the above elements, when tasked to an outside agency, will add an element of cost that will need to be covered when setting the finished price for your book. Each of the above elements that you undertake yourself will negate that cost.

This is obvious and there should be no need to state the obvious, but it is also obvious that too many writers, under the guise of self-publishing, hand over the whole process to the first company that entices them with a glossy advert and promises of publishing glory. The result is a book that is often priced out of the market, or at least large portions of the market where it might achieve the dreamed of sales.

The above tasks are not above undertaking by any individual of average intelligence. You may not know how, but it is not above learning and modern technology brings the potential of doing it all yourself. And I mean all of it, from start to finish including each element of book production.

Even if you don't want to go that far, knowing what is involved in doing each element will allow you to judge whether the price quoted if fair or not. Then, each element you do feel able undertake yourself will still reduce your total cost of production. It's up to you how many of these tasks you undertake yourself, but as a publisher you need to know what is involved because then you will be able to judge whether the fee charged is fair or not.

Now we will look at each task in detail.

STORY EDITING

The task of editing falls into two distinct areas. The first is story editing.

The story editor, also called a consulting editor, or commissioning editor, is responsible for deciding whether the story works. Beginning, middle and end and whether it has a strong enough USP. They judge whether the bones of the story, the skeleton is strong enough to support the meat and muscle. They judge characterisation by asking questions. Do the characters have - character? Are they believable? Are the characters real enough for the reader to care what happens to them? Then, does the story hook the reader in from the first line and does it play them through the following chapters enough to keep them hooked? And of course, is there a potential market for the finished book and if so, what is the potential size of the market. And most important of all, if we go ahead, can we make a profit?

Here lies the crux of the first problem for new authors. These judgements will be made on the criteria set by each particular publishing house and they will vary from publisher to publisher. One publisher will consider a book has no potential, another will consider it more viable. One editor will not be interested and excited by the content of a story while another will find it just what they like.

People are the same all over. Some like the style of one author and not another. We all have our own favourite authors and those we find difficult to read. I can name more than one famous author, with a high number of best selling books to their credit, yet I just don't read them. This doesn't mean they are not good writers. There is no accounting for taste and you cannot please everyone, so you must settle for pleasing those you can and trust there is enough to make your book a best seller.

Story editing is a matter of opinion. However, it is also a matter of opinion based on knowledge and a great deal of experience in what sells and a good editor tries to put aside personal preference in making any judgement on story quality. It's a question of hats, editing a manuscript is a different task from reading a book for pleasure. As is writing a book from publishing a book as is writing from editing.

In editing their own work the author has to overcome the hurdle of knowing what they mean to say when comparing this with what they've actually said. This is because the mind can automatically gloss over what's actually written and subconsciously replace it what should be written. It requires specific effort and concentration and there are a few tricks that help.

To avoid the trap of reading the story, sentence after sentence, by which mistakes can be missed, read each sentence, then read that sentence backwards before moving onto the next. When you get to the end of the paragraph, go back and read the whole paragraph then retrace that backwards before moving onto the next.

Mistakes can often be missed when editing onscreen so to avoid this, work on a printed copy of your manuscript. If editing onscreen, enlarge the print way beyond what you would normally use. Zoom in so each sentence fills the screen.

Take note that editing and rewriting are two different tasks. An editor does not make changes to text so nor should you. Mark any mistakes or changes, suggesting what those changes should be in the margin for the author to consider and confirm later. Then, if self-editing, go back later, change hats and make these changes. Publisher's hat, editor's hat, author's hat!

USE A RED PEN and take the time to learn and use the proper editing marks. Mistakes and suggested changes are marked using a red pen. If working on screen many applications will also allow you to mark suggested changes in red. If you are going to self-edit you want to do it properly and professionally, do you not?

An editor will commonly read the novel from start to finish to gain a basic understanding of the work and despite that you know the story and have probably read through and re-written a number of times, it is still advisable to read it through, as any other novel, not making changes, not even marking mistakes, then go through and edit.

DO NOT rely on the computer spell and grammar checker to check spelling and grammar.

DO refer to a dictionary, thesaurus and guides on grammar and English usage etc. It is better to take a few moments to check a questionable construction than let a mistake get by.

Remember that it is the story editor's task is to examine the different elements of a novel and then decide whether each element serves its purpose. Each element should then coalesce together to create a whole.

It is not the story editor's task to correct basic spelling and grammar despite this being a common expectation among some writers. The author should ensure that spelling and the grammatical construction of each sentence is correct. The editor may suggest an alternative construction and the use of alternative words where one is repeated a number of times, though the less the editor has to do the happier they will be.

The Elements of Novel.

The Plot:

This is the main point of conflict, the why of the story. The main character has, for whatever reason, to achieve a certain objective. The protagonist has, for whatever reason, to prevent the hero achieving that objective. The protagonist does not have to be an individual. It can be a situation or anything you care to imagine, but will commonly be defined by individuals promoting that situation.

You should be able to define the plot in a single sentence.

Sub-plots:

The same principle applies as with the main plot. Sub-plots may centre on the same hero-protagonist relationship, or may involve a third party such as the hero / romantic interest relationship, or maybe centre on completely different character groups running parallel but somehow embroiled and coming to a conjunction with main plot.

A sub-plot can be viewed as a story within a story and with care; it should be possible to view a sub-plot as a stand-alone story.

The Story:

The story is the account of how the plot develops, plays out and is resolved. Beginning, middle and end. How this is achieved will vary from writer to writer and is essentially, the writer's style. There is no right, but there is no end of wrongs. The word, subjective applies. The editor needs to be convinced the story is right and avoids the wrongs.

The difficulty in self-editing is that as the writer you are automatically convinced it is right. It is your baby. You are naturally protective. You need to keep an open mind and really work at being self-critical to self-edit with any degree of success.

The Beginning:

The starting point of the story does not have to be a huge event full of action. The following example is deliberately un-dramatic:

(The hero) tore open the letter, read the contents, then moved to the window, crumpling the paper in their hand as they gazed at the distant storm lashed mountains.

The mountain view insinuates that the setting is not in a city and there is a question put in the reader's mind. What is in the letter? The hero crumples it in their hand so it's obviously something disturbing. To find the answer, the reader must read on.

This is commonly called, the hook. As with fishing, the idea is that the writer needs to hook the reader into the story. This is done by raising a question in the readers mind. Why, who, what, when, where? This trigger event auger something that can only be explained by reading on, but it doesn't stop here. As one subjective question is answered, another is created resulting in a host of overlapping puzzles. How does the hero get out of a situation? Does the hero discover they are being tricked? The hook can be dramatic, zany, funny, romantic, and full of action, in fact anything but whatever it is it needs to intrigue to the reader. The result is a story the reader doesn't want to put down.

The opening paragraphs to The Mill on the Floss are pure descriptive prose. Nothing happens, it is just a description of the scene. The description raises the question of why it is given but even so, does not comply with the principle of the dramatic hook. Instead it uses the principle of intriguing the reader in a more literary manner.

This is the crux of the matter. You cannot please everyone. Nobody can write a book that satisfies every taste leaving the question of what makes a good book as much of a mystery as before. We're back to different hats. As a publisher, a good book is simply a book that sells enough copies for the publisher to make a huge profit. Yet most editors would rather publish a good literary book than a good mercenary book, which is why many move on to start a new independent small press publishing house, which is one reason why small independent publishers are accepted and respected in the market.

The Middle:

The body or middle of the story carries the story

forward. However, someone once said that the elements of a story are the beginning, the muddle and the end. I prefer the muddle because you don't want the reader to know what's going to happen next. You want the story to twist and turn. You want to keep the reader interested, so the main plot is expanded, sub-plots are introduced, and the characters are given substance. The story is developing towards the crescendo at the end, but the reader won't know how that crescendo will pan out.

Even so, the story must move at a pace.

Every story happens somewhere but long adjectival descriptions of location slow the pace and should be kept to the absolute minimum.

Every story happens at sometime, past, present or future, but even science fantasy has to follow a logical path. An awareness of technological availability comes into play. A pirate story manuscript I was given to edit had the ship move from the African Coast, to the Indies, to the coast of England at a pace that would test a modern cruise liner when in reality, such a voyage under sail may have taken a year or more. Nor can you have a character wearing a mini skirt before miniskirts were invented.

Every story involves an individual. The first rule with character development is that the characters you create must have character. The second rule in character development is that you must not have your character act out of character.

A story can be plot led or character led, but in a plot led story, it is a mistake to believe the above principle does not apply. A plot led story might not involve a single lead character, but the characters that appear in each element of the story must still comply with the principle requirement of characterisation. The reader must care.

One of the ways an author can achieve this is to create a back-story for each of their main characters. The back-story is a brief biography starts with the character's parents. However, it is an exercise in characterisation that doesn't appear in the actual story. Elements may be included, if there is a specific need to describe the motivation for some act by that character but otherwise; this exercise is a writing tool and nothing more.

So, where and when was the character born? Who were their parents and what did they do? Where did the character go to school? When was their first romantic entanglement and with who? An individual's character is defined, at least in part, by their upbringing and events that happened during their early life. Knowing this helps the author to apply consistency to their characterisation and helps to avoid having them do anything out of character.

A fault to watch for involves the appearance of secondary characters. Every story has secondary characters and these appear and disappear, sometimes violently, but whether they are named or not, all must be for a purpose. The fault is when they appear for no purpose. For example: In a scene from a detective story, the detective and his sergeant pull up in the car outside a bar.

Ed (the sergeant) winced as the inspector slammed the door, watched as he straightened his raincoat before entering the bar. He then turned back to watching the street.

Murphy (the detective) looked around the near empty bar, his eyes fixing on the barman nonchalantly wiping a glass with a grubby cloth. He walked to the bar feeling it sticky with the residue of countless spilt drinks.

Murphy flashed his badge. *'This your place?'*
'Yeh.'
'Your name?'
'Why?'
'There's my badge and my name on it. See. Detective Murphy. So you know my name. What's yours? There was an obvious threat in Murphy's tone.

'Brice,' the bar owner replied. *'Tom Brice.'*
'Well Mr Brice, I'm looking for someone called Caxton. (an informant) *I heard he drinks in here.'*
'Ain't seen 'im. 'E ain't been in for weeks, Brice lied.'
'Yeh. Well call me if he comes in.'
'Sure Inspector.'

Murphy turned, walked out and got back in the car. *'He's not there.'* Murphy put the car in gear and headed to the next bar.

Not a bad scene overall, but why give him a name? This creates an impression that he is of some relevance to the story, that he plays a role somewhere in the plot, but reading on, this is the only scene where this barman appears. So why introduce a character when they serve no further purpose? In addition, character introduction interrupts the flow discovering that they do not will disappoint this expectation.

Alternatively, the barman character can be justified by adding, after the detective left:

Another fault I that there must always be a logical way out of any situation. If a thousand villains with no chance to escape surround the hero, the invention of a pure chance occurrence that lets the hero escape will leave the reader severely dissatisfied. However, seeming impossible methods of escape, however fantastical, can work if sufficiently presaged in previous scenes.

All action must also serve a purpose. In one scene I was editing recently, the hero was questioning a minor character. The character then started fumbling in their bag, creating the expectation that this was relevant to the action, but no. The conversation ended, they separate, so why did they fumble in their bag? Speaking to the author later, they revealed that they wanted to indicate that this minor character was nervous. The author could see it clearly in their mind and it appeared to make perfect sense, except the reader is not a mind reader. They will infer so far, but only with enough information to do so.

Of course the reader will want some clue to character description and this is where we come to the difference between showing and telling. Telling is writing a long descriptive passage such as, *'he was tall and handsome with blue eyes and neatly cut brown hair'* but where possible, it is better to show such descriptions by incorporating such them into the flow of the story.

For example:

Writing: *'The Captain had a wooden leg'* is the author telling the reader this piece of information, but interrupts the pace of the story.

Writing: *'The Captain stamped his wooden leg on the deck'* incorporates this same descriptive information into the action of the story without interrupting the pace.

Pace is important. An editor will want to see the story moving inexorably forward. The pace should vary but not be allowed to stop and stagnate in long sections of descriptive prose.

An editor will also be on the watch for author intrusion.

The author naturally intrudes because the author is the one who create the characters and narrates the story. For this reason, a certain element of the author's character and opinion will naturally impose itself on those characters and the theme of the story. This occurs more so when writing in first person as the author often takes on the role of the character they create. However, author intrusion will still stand out for the following reasons.

Author intrusion is where the author imposes too much of their opinion on that of the character and in so doing, the character acts in a way the author would act and not as the character would be expected to act.

Author intrusion is also revealed by descriptions or revelation of knowledge that isn't consistent within the context of the story.

Author intrusion is also shown when the dialogue appears directed towards the reader rather than being contained within the action of the story.

The use of dialogue is an important factor to consider in editing. Another aspect of showing and telling is that descriptive elements of the story can be shown through character dialogue. For example:

Sally walked in wearing a red dress.

or

 'Wow!' Tom said. 'That dress, it's so red!'

They looked at the sheer cliff wondering how they could possible climb it.

or

'How do we climb that? It's so steep?'

Another issue in the use of dialogue is the use of, he

said - she said addition. This should be limited to the absolute minimum required to inform the reader who is speaking. Remember that the reader is not stupid. The use of opening and closing quotation, or speech marks, indicates who is speaking. Speech marks close when tone character finishes speaking. Move to a new line, new speech marks open when a the other character begins speaking.

Another fault is adding 'ily' words after, 'he said - she said', as in: 'Don't you ever do that again,' he said angrily. The mood of the individual speaking should be revealed by the expressive nature of the dialogue or some form of action:

He slammed his fist onto the table. 'Don't you ever do that again,' he said.

Is it or is it not obvious that the individual speaking is angry? Next, question whether the addition of 'he said' is necessary. If not, cut it out because every time you write, he/she said, you interrupt the pace and spoil the flow.

Remember that it is more difficult to write a short passage than a long one. Excess verbiage and adjectival decoration should be avoided, but the defining word here is, excess. The judgement between what is excess and what is necessary to add colour to the story is a matter of personal taste and opinion.

As an exercise, cut a sentence down to the bare bones

of what needs to be said, the John has a cat exercise.

Now consider all the different ways this basic piece of information can be conveyed to the reader:

That's John's cat - The cat belongs to John - John owns that cat - and so on.

This is a black and white statement. There is no colour; no added description other than John has a cat. Add in one descriptive element such as, John has a black cat and consider the possible variations. Any added description adds a basic level of interest to a statement, but take it a step further. John has a black cat with a ragged ear. Fair enough, but does the fact that the cat also has a ragged ear have any particular relevance to the story? Does this ragged ear play a role, or is it just added description. You may like that added description or you may consider it excess verbiage because it serves no purpose. This is where the author has a choice. An editor may wish to cut; the author may insist the description stays. It's your choice.

This conflict can be compared to fashion and design and literary fashion changes as any other. Keep in mind that modern literary fashion is more minimalist than the prose of Dickens, that said, a story will become bland and uninteresting unless some literary colour is added. Applying the above exercise to the written word helps to identify what is necessary to carry the story forward and what is necessary to colour the literary picture being created. How far this goes is down to personal opinion

The End

The hero wins, the villain gets his comeuppance and there should be no loose ends, no sub-plots left unresolved and the reader must be satisfied with the way these events are resolved. However, it is permissible to leave some unresolved issues if the same characters are going to be carried forward into a subsequent story.

Copyediting is something different.

COPY-EDITING

Copy-editing is also called line editing, or sub-editing, often leading to the mistaken belief that this is somewhat less than story editing. Copyediting is not concerned with the literary quality of the story, but with the technical rules of grammatical construction.

A number of books commonly found on the working author's bookshelf, English Usage, English Grammar, The Plain English Guide, Usage and Abusage and so on, provide guidance on grammatical construction. If these tools were used, as they should be, the copy editor would have far less work to do, but here we come to the Startrek conundrum.

Each episode begins with the announcement: 'To boldly go where no man has gone before,' which sends most copy editors into an apoplectic fit of rage because it breaks a grammatical rule by splitting the infinitive, to - go. The alternative, To go boldly where no man has gone before, is no better leaving, To go where no man has gone before boldly, is the only grammatically correct version. But this is clunky and few writers will be satisfied with this form of words. The statement could be changed to, Boldly going where no man has gone before, but this changes the tense from future to present and here you have the conundrum, what is right in one way is wrong in another and the result is a need to compromise.

I will add another issue, that of beginning a sentence with a conjunction, 'and' 'but' etc. as above. Some copy-editors will view this as beyond the pale while others will accept that the use of language is continually evolving and such usage is now becoming quite commonplace.

A good writer will attempt, at all times, to comply with the rules of grammatical construction, but literary principle will often take president. Or should that be: At all times, a good writer will attempt to comply with the rules of grammatical construction. Or maybe: A good writer will attempt, to comply with the rules of grammatical construction at all times.

A good copy editor insists on applying the rules of grammatical construction while tempering this insistence with an element of literary licence. A good writer, attempting to be a good copy editor, will examine the construction of each sentence and each element of that sentence, each stop, each comma, each phrase and as a copy-editor, wearing a copy-editor's hat, will mark that word/phrase for correction then move on to examine the next line. As with the story editor, changes are not made during the editing process. Whether to accept and make those *suggested* changes is the writer's task, but the writer should also have the good sense to accept grammatical correction where needed.

Another element is Copy-editing relates to the publisher's style sheet. The use of English grammar allows for a number of variables in punctuation, spelling, capitalisation and so on. For example, speech or quotation marks may be double " or single '. A publisher's style sheet as found with newspapers and magazines, will dictate their preferred style with the aim of maintaining consistency in presentation. This same principle applies in book publishing, the aim being consistency in presentation. Help is available from publications such as, Strunk and White's Elements of Style.

William Strunk Jnr taught English at Cornell University and E. B White is the author of Charlotte's Web and Stuart Little. William Strunk wrote the original as a guide for his students to use and E.B. White revised this to become the accepted guide it is now.

Strunk & White's Elements of Style does indeed provide some valuable guidance and advice on various aspects of sentence construction but, as with all things, there are those that contest some of the points made in this guide and prefer one of the many others. The ACS Style Guide, the AMA Manual of Style, The Chicago Manual of Style, the AP Guide, the ASA Guide, Fowlers, the list goes on with every country having its own list of preferred style guides.

However, whether you use a guide or not, the key issue is consistency. For example: The question whether you use double or single quotation marks for dialogue is not important. What is important is that you use the same quotation marks throughout your manuscript. The style and format you se in one place, you use in every place. Consistency is the issue.

The Building Blocks of a Sentence

Sentences are constructed from subject verb pairings called, clauses. The number and type of clauses from which a sentence is constructed determine the grammatical classification of a sentence. A sentence with a single subject verb pairing is called, simple. This does not mean short. A simple sentence can contain compound main elements and long modifying phrases and still be classed as simple. The number of verb pairings defines the nature of the sentence. To be defined as complex, the sentence must include at least one additional dependent clause. A compound sentence lacks the additional dependent clause but has at least two independent clauses usually joined by a connective, and, but, nor, yet or a comma or semicolon.

The basic rule for the construction of a sentence is that the verb comes after the subject and before the object. This requires the ability to differentiate between the subject and object in a sentence and the subject is not necessarily what the sentence is about. For example: I find fishing boring. The sentence is about fishing being boring, but the subject is 'I'.

The subject of a sentence can be found by asking to whom or what does the verb apply. The verb is *finds*, so who or what *finds*?

A sentence, as an expression of a complete thought, can be constructed using a subject and a verb: Pilots fly. An object is added to round out the though: Pilots fly planes. The object is the physical action conveyed by the verb.

A transitive verb is one that has a receiver for its action. A verb that has no receiver for its action is called intransitive. Some verbs are naturally transitive or intransitive while others can be either, depending on their use. A transitive verb can be in used either the passive or active voice however it is always the subject that is active or passive. The term voice designates whether the subject is acting or being acted upon: Pilots fly planes - Planes are flown by pilots.

The difference between the direct and indirect object in a sentence depends on its construction: Pilots give students advice. The indirect object is the word directly after the verb. The sentence can be turned around by swopping direct and indirect objects: Pilots give advice to students. The indirect object and subject can also be switched: Students are given advice by pilots, which is a grammatical twist where the passive voice takes an object. The subject of the passive verb does not receive the action of the verb, but the object of that action and is called, within grammatical circles, a retained object.

Are you totally baffled yet? The purpose of this chapter is to instil in the author the difficulty of self-editing as it should be done and here, I am only skimming the subject. However, I am also outlining some of the main points to look for so that if you insist on doing it yourself, you will have at least some understanding of what to look for. Read on.

While the majority of sentences require this subject verb pairing to be classified as simple or complex, there are a few allowable word groups that are treated as a sentence despite having no verb. These commonly appear in dialogue as an expression or single word answer to a question. Yes. No. Wow! And a few others.

By now you are feeling a combination of boredom and confusion and probably want to have nothing more to do with copy-editing. However, it doesn't need to be that difficult. It is a question of looking at the sentence. The biggest fault made by writers in self-editing is reading the sentence instead of looking at and examining the method of its construction.

In reading, the majority of people recognise word shapes and even the shape of word groupings. They therefore skim over the grammatical construction and even miss obvious spelling mistakes. Admit it. We all do it and you will still find mistakes in mainstream published novels that have escaped the editor. (Can you spot the potential error in this last sentence? Answer to come shortly.)

Fat and Flabby Sentences

The purpose of a sentence is to convey information, but what information does it *need* to convey. The word *need* is key. Is this information relevant, important, required, or is it superfluous to what is needed?

John has a black cat, is a straightforward conveyance of information. John has a spiteful black cat, adds to that information, but does the reader need to also know that the cat is spiteful. Does this information hold any specific relevance to a later aspect of the story? I.e. Does the cat later do something that justifies the information of it being spiteful?

The purpose of a sentence is to convey information but conveying information that has no purpose distracts from the importance of the information that does.

Fat and flabby sentences are those containing weak verbs, abstract words, ponderous nouns and rambling modifiers. From an editor's perspective, the problem is that writers are notorious for failing to trust a word to do its job, or maybe failing to allow that the reader has enough intelligence to understand without covering every element of that information in detail.

For example: Consider the sentence: *He finally arrived at the top of the hill*. His arrival at the top of the hill is the final part of the journey anyway so why add finally? The writer has either not trusted the word arrived or added finally as padding, a make weight to expand the word count of the manuscript, something story all editors have seen before.

Another phrase that commonly crops up is, *consensus of opinion*, however, the word *consensus* means, *agreement of opinion*. Therefore the phrase, *consensus of opinion* means, *consensus of opinion of opinion*. Yet time after time this phrase continues to appear.

The statement that it is much harder to write a short story, say 600 words, than a long one, is true and every writer should accept the challenge of trying to write ultra short stories.

The task is to cut the sentence back to its bare bones, so that it contains only the basic information that needs to be conveyed. Imagine that every word costs a £1 or $1. Get a stack of coins and put one in a pot for every word you use.

But an anorexic sentence is as bad as a fat and flabby one. The trick in writing is to start with the bare minimum, the bones, and the skeleton of the sentence and then add the flesh. Enough decoration can be added to make it sparkle, but not so much that the glitz dazzles the reader and overwhelms the information that needs to be conveyed. An editor, faced with a fat sentence, will be like a surgeon faced with an obese patient. The risk is that they suck the guts out of it.

So, to cut or not to cut, that is the question. A copy editor's task is not an easy one. It requires not only an understanding of the mechanics of sentence but also an understanding of literary prose and licence.

Faulty Connections

The principle of sentence construction is that the verb normally comes after the subject and before the object and modifiers normally go next to the elements they qualify. The connection between verb, subject, object and modifiers can become jumbled and when this occurs, the reader can become confused. Compare the following.

We all do it and you will still find mistakes in mainstream published novels that have escaped the editor.

Or should that be:

We all do it and you will still find mistakes that have escaped the editor in mainstream published novels.

Alternatively:

We all do it and in mainstream published novels you will still find mistakes that have escaped the editor.

The principle is that when words aren't near the words they are meant to go with, they go with the words they are near. Potential problems such as this can be avoided by altering the construction but first, they have to be spotted and this becomes very difficult when self-editing simply because you know what you mean. The eventual reader doesn't. They need to discern the meaning from what you've written, so make sure you write what you mean to say.

Modifiers

A modifier is a word, phrase or clause that adds information about its subject. *The plane with the red wing.* The phrase, *the red wing* adds information about the plane. All very simple except that modifying phrases can become disjointed from the subject they modify:

Sally found Simon's desire to do that amusing.

The word *amusing* modifies the adjective *desire*, but the word *amusing* cannot follow the word it modifies because the infinitive phrase *to do* that takes that place. The sentence needs reconstructing:

Sally was amused by Simon's desire to do that.

You may choose to stress and adjective by putting it first in a sentence:

Amused by Simon's desire to do that, Sally...

A more obvious example of this comes from the 'wants' column in a local newspaper:

Could anyone please donate a wheelchair, electric or pushed by someone no longer needed?

The modifying phrase, *no longer needed*, should apply to the wheelchair, but here it appears to apply to the person doing the pushing.

Adverbs

Adverbs generally fall into the correct position automatically, but adverbs not only modify verbs. They can grammatically modify verbals, adjectives, other adverbs and even whole sentences. Having said that, the purpose of this chapter is to illustrate some of the basic principles in copy-editing; it is not to cover the whole subject in detail. Discussing every potential for misplaced modifiers would require pages alone. Add the subjects of parallelism, subject verb disagreement, punctuation, a chapter on the use of commas alone, and you have a completely different book.

Thankfully there are books on the subject so the rest of this chapter will be limited to some general principles.

A Few General Rules

Weak verbs in sentence openings put the brakes on that sentence at the moment it is meant to be accelerating. Compare the following two examples of saying the same thing: *There is a quick way of doing it, which is to ...* or: *A quick way of doing it is to...* The second version serves the same purpose with no detriment to the meaning.

Look for nouns or adjectives stuck in a weak verb/ preposition sandwiches. Phrases such as: *is able to do* and *Can make use of* can easily become just *can* and *use*.

Converting prepositional phrases to an active verb is easy and always beneficial. In the same way, a noun ending in *'tion'* can be changed to the *'ing'* form of a verb; *discussion* becomes *discussing* and therefore more active. A prepositional phrase such as: *of vital importance*, can be converted to: *vitally important*.

Weak words will attract needless words to prop them up. Needless words then obscure the correct interpretation and understanding of a sentence. This can also occur when words are out of place, a problem that mostly occurs in the use of modifiers within the sentence.

Punctuation

And here is a can of worms mentioned before but worth repeating. Some grammarphobes will have a fit over starting a sentence with *and*, yet happily begin a sentence with *but,* also a conjunction. This argument will go on and on and is just one of the decisions the editor and author will need to make.

As stated previously, writing evolves and so must the rules of grammar, but I would argue that the modern trend towards the abolition of all punctuation is a step too far. Punctuation serves the very specific purpose of clarifying sentence construction. This can add substance and more importantly, prevent misreading. To complicate matters, some style manuals promote the use to commas and other punctuations marks while others promote their avoidance.

Here is a list of some of the most common punctuation mistakes.

The Comma

The comma is used between adjectives where each qualifies as a noun: *She was a happy, joyful girl,* but not where one adjective qualifies the other. *A bright blue dress.*

Commas are used to separate items in a list: *Fish, chips and peas.* At this point, some will argue that there should also be a comma after chips. Others will argue vehemently that there should not. A publisher's style sheet will dictate that publisher's preference.

A comma marks the beginning and end of an inserted word or phrase: *Paul, who owns the blue car, didn't want to drive.*

A comma is use to separate a phrase or subordinate clause from a clause where misunderstanding is possible: *In the valley below, the villages looked very small.* Consider this sentence without the comma. First the phrase: *In the valley below the villages...* So the valley is below the villages, but then the phrase: *looked very small.* Any minor confusion interrupts the flow and spoils reader enjoyment. While inserting a comma is one solution, a better solution might be better to alter the sentence construction to avoid any potential misunderstanding.

In addition, a comma can also be inserted where the writer wants to force the reader to pause.

The origin of writing is that all early writing was designed to be read; this is because the vast majority of people were unable to read. The origin of punctuation was to indicate places where the reader should pause for breath, or add emphasis etc. As a rule, the comma indicates a pause for the count of 1 while a semicolon indicates a pause for a count of 2.

Note though that a comma should not be used to separate a subject from its predicate, or a verb from an object that is a clause.

Semicolon

A semicolon is used to indicate a more distinct break between parts of a sentence than indicated by a comma, but where these parts are connected too closely to be made into different sentences. That said, the writer has the right to choose. Consider the early sentence:

The origin of writing is that all early writing was designed to be read; this is because the vast majority of people were unable to read.

Or:

The origin of writing is that all early writing was designed to be read. This is because the vast majority of people were unable to read.

And yes, there are elements here that the MS Word spellcheck will argue is *passive voice*. Other spellcheckers will not, but no writer and especially no editor should rely on any computer spell and grammar checker to do their job. The question is: Does the sentence clearly and concisely convey the information the writer wants to convey despite ignoring the nuances of grammatical perfection?

Exclamation Mark.

The exclamation mark is usually taken to apply as a concluding full stop, but this is not necessarily so, despite what the computer spell check might argue. An exclamation mark is used to show an exclamatory word of phrase and before the invention of the typewriter, writers would use an exclamation mark, without the stop mark underneath, anywhere within a sentence. The limitations of the qwerty keyboard saw the demise of this usage.

Using an exclamation mark should be very simply but one mistake that keeps appearing is illustrated in the statement: *Wow! John exclaimed.* The exclamation mark tells the reader that *Wow!* is an exclamation. *Writing Wow! John Exclaimed* is the equivalent of saying, *Wow John Exclaimed John exclaimed.* Either you tell the reader John exclaimed in words or you use an exclamation mark, not both. Better still have the person exclaiming do something active: *Wow! John jumped from his seat...*

Faulty Agreement

The subject and its verb must both be single or plural, not single subject with plural verb or vice versa.

Pronouns must agree with each other.

Fragmentary Sentences

A complete sentence must contain both a subject and a verb. The subject is who or what. The verb says something about the subject. A fragmentary sentence is a phrase or group of words presented as a sentence but without the required subject verb combination.

Fused Sentences

A sentence should express only one central idea. A sentence may contain any number of subordinate clauses linked to this central idea, but these should not fuse into a second central idea.

Passive Voice

Active verbs are more direct and less wordy than passive verbs. Remember that weak verbs always require other words in support.

It is by using this equation that the answer to the question will be calculated. (Passive)

This equation will calculate the answer to the question. (Active)

Vague Pronouns

Ensure that pronouns such as 'it - this' and 'they' refer to something specific. Beginning a sentence with 'It is...' and 'they are...' when referring to something previous can create confusion with the reader trying to judge what 'It' or 'They' refer to.

Dangling Modifiers

Modifiers cannot only be misplaced; they can be left dangling so that it isn't clear what they modify.

When not going to work, my hobbies range from golf to fishing.

This construction insinuates that the hobbies go to work. This should be:

When I am not going to work, my hobbies range from gold to fishing.

Mixed Metaphors

Metaphors add colour to your writing but consider the literal meaning of any metaphor you use as faulty or mixed metaphors can create an unintended visual image in the readers mind.

Wordiness and Word Faults

Don't use fancy words to appear clever. Don't add words. See Fat and Flabby sentences. Use a dictionary to confirm word meaning.

There is more. There is so much more, so if you do insist on self-editing, do invest in a book on the subject, or even several. Two I have on my shelf are: Line by Line by Claire Kehrwald Cook and, Revision and Self-Editing by James Scott Bell, plus Usage and Abusage, the Plain English Guide, English Usage, Oxford English Grammar and many more. Just as a carpenter will have a hammer and a saw, these books are the tools of the trade of a writer and editor, but it is not enough to just have them, you need to use them.

A Few Tips on the Physical Aspects of Editing

You method you use to edit is subject to personal preference. I recommend using a hard copy instead of editing on screen. If you do, ensure the print is double-spaced.

It is easier to spot mistakes when working with text printed in a sans font than text printed in a serif font. Serif fonts are those with the small tails or widening at the end of each letter stroke, such as Times New Roman. The human eye tends to pick up mistakes easier when looking at a sans font than a serif font.

Place a ruler or blank sheet of paper under each line. Read the line and then read the line backwards. Then going forward again examining each word, each phrase before moving to the next line. When you get to the end of a sentence, read that sentence again, but not simply reading. Make the effort to analyse its structure and exactly what it says. Consider other ways of presenting the same information. Ask the question, are there any words that serve no purpose. If so, can they be cut?

Follow the same process when you get to the end of each paragraph and yes, this process requires effort and concentration, especially at the beginning, but it becomes easier with practice.

If editing on screen zoom in and enlarge the text, then use the curser to highlight the line you are editing. Follow the same procedure as with editing a printed copy only using the curser to highlight each line, sentence and paragraph as you proceed. You may wish to change the highlight colour or enlarge or change the font for each section as you proceed. The trick is to ensure the section you are working on stands out as this helps to prevent the eye wandering onward before seeing any mistakes or needed corrections.

Mistakes should be marked with a red pen, or highlighted on screen by, for example, changing that element of text to red, for the writer to correct later.

You won't though. You will begin to do corrections as you proceed, so ensure that once you have done those corrections, go back and re-edit.

Some modern word-processing applications allow easy reversion of editing changes, but I recommend keeping a pre-edited back-up version of all manuscripts. While working on a manuscript, there is no problem with keeping several versions that can be referred to or used to reconstitute elements you later regret cutting out. Problems arise by not having an older version to fall back on if ever you find the need.

Copyediting is a task you can undertake yourself but it must not be undertaken lightly. It requires doing properly and doing it properly requires effort. This is why editors charge what they do and you can only justify saving this cost if you apply an equal standard when doing it yourself.

TEXT FILE PREPARATION

So now you have an edited manuscript file and are ready to move onto production, but before you do there are some elements of the process that are easier to prepare prior of uploading and there are also some ways of working that cause problems and extra work when it comes to the actual book design.

If you plan to publish as an e-book, the e-publishing service will provide you with a choice of templates and full instructions on how to do this. Note that different e-book formats have different requirements. For a physical book, the choice is between using a print on demand system, or a genuine book production service, but always beware the vanity trap.

Most physical book design is done using a DTP (Desk Top Publishing) application. The book is designed and then converted to a PDF (Portable Document Format) file. As the publisher you can contract out this task to a book design service or do it yourself, but more on this later.

As stated at the start, some elements of file preparation are easier to do before transferring to a book design application and some word-processing format options can cause a great deal of addition work.

Page Break

You need to remember that your manuscript needs to be reformatted to fit the page size and design of a finished book. The page size will be different from the standard A4 layout used by most text file word-processor applications. A common fault is that some people use the return key to move the cursor down to a new page when starting a new chapter. When the text is transferred to a different page format, doing this will create unwanted line breaks within the text. Even tapping the return key two or three times at the end of a chapter can result in the same problem. Your new chapter should begin on the very next line after the end of the previous chapter. Then use the Page Break option to transfer that first line to a new page. The Page Break option in Word is in the Insert menu.

Always ensure the curser is at the next line after the last line of the text. Then use page break option to start the next chapter on a new page.

Paragraph Indents

Some people use the space bar to set their first line paragraph indents. Others use the TAB setting to create these indents. Using TAB for paragraph indents can result in the appearance of a double indent in your transferred file. Both are bad practice and the people that do this are regularly cursed by those given the task of formatting their manuscript because it is a long boring process to go through a whole novel to remove these unwanted letter or tab indents.

First line indents at the beginning of a new paragraph or text break should always be formed using the *Indent* facility in the format menu. This will then transfer and correspond to the indent facility of your DTP or e.pub application. Alternatively, all correctly applied but unwanted formatting can be easily cleared by using the Clear All Formatting option or by a file transferring trick known to most editors and book designers.

Never use the tab or spacebar to set paragraph indents.

Font or Typeface Selection

The generic word processing font is Times New Roman, but very few books are published using Times New Roman. Some in the publishing profession consider using Times New Roman as a sign of a self-published book. The font you choose is more important than you might think.

Fonts come in a wide range of styles and designs, but some fonts are classed as *Open Type* and others as *Closed Type*. In book design, Open Type is best. Open Type fonts contain optional style sets that create ligatures, drop characters and other design tweaks that improve the look of a page.

Ligatures join certain letter combinations together and can be switched on and off when using high quality typesetting applications.

For example: In the word fire, in some typefaces, the dot over the letter *i* almost collides with the curved top for the letter *f*. A good typeface replaces the dot over the letter *i* with a ligature joining it to the line through the letter *f*.

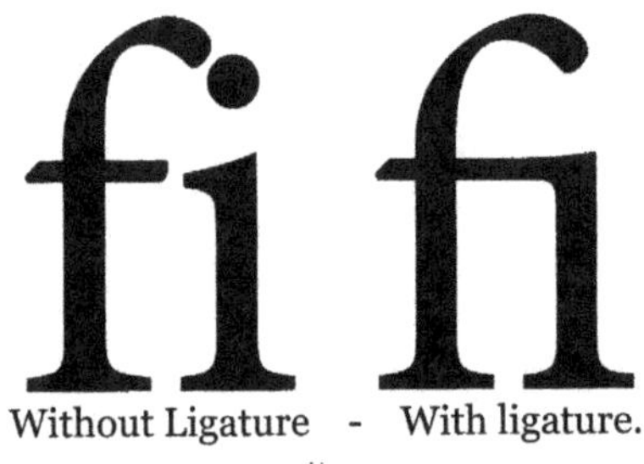

Without Ligature - With ligature.

Drop characters are certain letters that when they appear as the first capital letter of a sentence or paragraph, the base of this character falls below the line of text, in line with the bottom of the small letter g or y.

Ligatures and other stylistic adjustments, available when using Open Type fonts, may not appear visible unless you know what you are looking for, but they do improve the overall appearance of the printed page and book design and page layout is all about appearance.

Note. It is usually easier to change a word processing file

to the font you want to use than try and do this when formatting in a DTP application. Select the font your want to use and make this change before transferring your file.

Line Spacing

Most writers work using the double space line setting but most books are not double-spaced. Most DTP applications allow you to set your line spacing by the millimetre. Word will allow it by the text point using the exact facility. Other applications, such as Scrivener will also allow this millimetre setting.

Reverting to single or required line spacing prior to transferring is generally easier beforehand.

Chapter Headings & Sub-heads.

Chapter headings, even when this is simply, Chapter 1, Chapter 2 etc., can result in problems.

Word processing files generally have the ability to select and format Body Text, Headers and Sub-headers separately. Lazy writers often ignore this, using the text format to enlarge the font, centre, embolden etc. They also use the space bar to force however many blank lines they want between the headline and the first line of text and all these blank lines, for various reasons, can result in further problems.

When laying out a book, it is important to have the

same space, between the chapter heading and the first line of text, for every chapter. Writers have a tendency to put 5 line returns on one chapter, 6 on another, and 4 somewhere else. Also, these line returns can vary depending on the applicable font size at the time they are made.

Word processing applications have a header, sub head facility for a reason. A word processing application is a tool. Use it properly or don't use it at all.

Page Numbers

Word Processing files allow for the insertion of page numbers, but this is the one element that will not be passed on for the simple reason that the volume of text per page will be different. This is as long as the Insert Page Number facility is used. Believe it or not, some people manually type each page number at the bottom of each page, making it part of the body text, which is transferred. The result is the appearance of these numbers at odd places throughout the DTP file, which then have to be manually removed.

The text format processes in word processing applications are there for a reason. Use them.

Digital Quirks

Finally something for which the writer cannot be blamed. Computers are not infallible and digital quirks can occur during text transfer from one application to another. This is the purpose of, Proof Reading, or at least one of the purposes and this will be covered later.

However, there is one digital quirk that can be prevented and this applies to e-publishing as much as any other.

In some cases during book design, the first and final letter in a line will appear to be cut vertically in half. Part of the letter may appear faded or cut away. This may happen to the first or last letter in every line on a page or just a selected few, but will only appear on the printed proof or on the e-book reader when the book file is opened to read. On screen the text will all be there and appear correct.

The cause is difficult to explain without getting technical and the correct digital solution can be to start fiddling with kern and letter space settings until the problem goes away. The easy solution is to use the indent settings and apply a 0.01cm indent setting to each margin to the body text throughout the whole document. This has been found to work in all the cases I have come across.

Some DTP applications will read and apply the formatting settings of your word processing file, some do not and some will apply some formatting but not all. For this reason the majority of designers like to clear all formatting then start again. However, this clear all formatting option will not get rid of indents created using the tab key of misuse of the space bar. Nor will it get rid of line spacing cause by misuse of the return key. Always use word processing format settings correctly as this will save you a great deal of time if doing the design yourself and a great deal of money if paying a design service to do it on your behalf.

THE PARTS OF A BOOK

First there are the physical parts of a book, which depend on the physical design, case bound or soft cover, perfect bound or stitched. Then there internal parts, the way the content is divided into different elements, each with its own specific purpose.

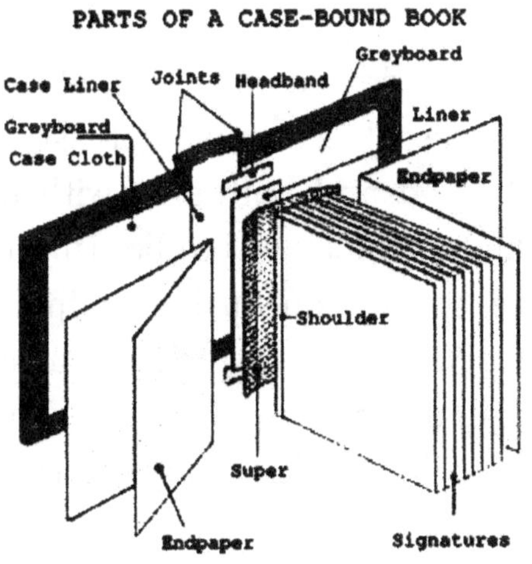

A case bound book consists of a hard cover constructed using two pieces of greyboard for the front and back and another thinner piece for the spine of case liner. These are covered and joined with case cloth, or with a durable printed paper cover. A space of approximately ¼" is left between the front and backboard and the case liner to form joints that allow the book to open. The case cloth is commonly printed with the title and author's name on gold block letters.

The page content of the book, called a bookblock, is made up of signatures. Pages are printed in multiples of four giving 4, 8, 16, 32, 64 pages per sheet, depending on the required size of the finished book and the size of the sheet used for printing. Each sheet is then folded into a signature. A signature usually consists of sixteen or thirty-two pages. perfect bound into a card cover and trimmed to size.

Each signature is stitched and cased, glued together using a super, made of loose weave cloth, strengthened with a liner, topped and bottomed with decorative headbands. The bookblock has to be trimmed before gluing into the cover, done using endpapers. Case bound books are commonly covered with an additional dust jacket, originally for the purpose its name implies but now usually printed with a cover illustration and used as a marketing tool.

Case bound book production used to be a long and laborious process, done by hand, using a manual book press, but as with everything, automated machinery does the job.

While commonly viewed as a single process, book production is actually two separate processes, printing being the first, print finishing being the second. There are companies that specialise in print finishing and this task may be done by a completely different company from the one that prints the book.

The production of perfect bound books is a lot simpler and therefore, a lot less expensive. Pages can be printed the same way, into signatures, then folded and placed together to form a book block. The bookblock is then glued into a pre-folded card cover and trimmed to size.

The type of glue used to form a bookblock can vary. The two main processes are, a padding process, using a padding press, where the pages for maybe ten or twenty books are stacked in a padding press. An acid free glue, usually PVA, is then applies to the binding edge and allowed to dry. The individual books are then separated, using a padding knife. Each glued bookblock is then glued into their cover and trimmed. Most modern automated binding systems now use a hot glue process, but padding remains a viable, if slower, method of book production.

Other binding methods are available, but the majority of books are either case bound or perfect bound.

The internal parts of a book are divided into three main elements, the front matter, the body and the back matter. The body of the book is its main content, the story. As their name indicates, the front matter appears at the front of the book, the back matter at the back of the book. These are both again subdivided into separate elements, each with its own purpose. It is not necessary to include each and every one of these elements as their use, or not, is a matter of personal choice and requirement though certain elements, such as the copyright page, must be included.

Front-Matter

Half Title

Also called the bastard title, because it only contains the title of the book, with no author name. If used, this appears on the first recto page when you open the book.

Frontpiece

An illustration on the verso facing the title page, sometimes the verso of the half title page.

Title Page

Announces the title, subtitle, author and publisher. Additional information may be included, such as the publisher's address, date of publication or even a short descriptive sentence. An illustration may also be included.

Copyright Page

Most important and usually on the verso of the title page. This carries the books ISBN number, copyright statement, publication and edition information, print history, legal notices, cataloguing data, credits for cover design and any internal artwork specific to the book, editing, production, contributors and any other official credit you wish to give.

Dedication

If a dedication is to be given, this appears after the copyright page, either facing or on the next page.

Epigraph

Some authors like to add a quotation or some other statement to their book, largely depending on the type of book.

Table of Contents or Contents Page

Usually on a recto page, this lists the parts or chapters in which the book is divided. More common in non-fiction than fiction unless each chapter is given its own sub-title.

The Body

The book's main content be it fiction or non-fiction.

The Back-Matter

Most back matter content is applicable to non-fiction than fiction, though some elements may apply.

Postscript

Anything added as an afterthought to the main body of the content.

Appendix or Addendum

Commonly only applicable in non-fiction. A supplement to the main content, maybe noting some recent discovery too late to include in the main content. Sometimes including source documents and research references.

Chronology

Can also be included in the front matter. Commonly applicable to historical non-fiction but can also apply to historical fiction.

Endnotes

These come after any appendices and are commonly divided by chapter to make their references clearer.

Glossary

An alphabetical list of terms and their definitions.

Bibliography

A list of books, articles and other works used as reference material and cited within the main body of the book.

List of Contributors

First and last name of each contributor, often including a brief biographical note of academic affiliation and previous publications.

Index

An alphabetical list of people, places, events, cited works along with the page number of where these references may be found.

Errata

A notice of an error within the content of the book, sometimes caused during the production process.

Colophon

This may credit the book's designer, the describe the typography, identify the typeface along with a brief history of its design.

The Cover

The cover of a book is obviously a different size from that of an internal page. Therefore the cover for your book will always be designed and created as a separate PDF file.

Most DTP applications provide suitable templates both for page and cover design and it is it is not difficult to do even from scratch. Further information on this subject provided later.

THE PRINCIPLES OF PAGE LAYOUT & BOOK DESIGN

So you've selected and edited, or had someone else edit, the manuscript you want to publish. This is where most self-publishers reply to one of the many publishing service and hand the whole task over to someone else, and it is at least one step too soon to do that.

The choices you face will depend on the format you intend to use to publish your book. This choice of format should depend on the market potential for the book, as discussed at the start of the process. Part of understanding the market potential revolves around the potential market value of the book, the potential retail price you can charge while allowing for any retail/distribution discount you will need to give. This gives you an allowable cost of production to aim for. As with all things, the more you can do yourself, the lower you can force the cost of production. One task you can do yourself is the design process.

Your book is most likely laid out in some word-processing format, or one of the new book-writing applications that bill themselves as allowing easy conversion the file to book layout format. Whatever these claims, the publisher has a choice. I wouldn't touch any vanity publisher with a bargepole, especially those that charge for creating an e-book because the main e-publishing platforms all provide their own set of templates and full instructions on their layout requirements and if you simply follow their instructions, you can easily do it yourself.

If you are looking to produce a physical book, the next step is to convert the manuscript from its word processing layout into the desired book design format.

Most book design is done using a DTP application and there are some genuine editorial and book design services that can do this for you and also some genuine book production services that also offer a design service, but always beware of the vanity vulture that regularly disguise themselves as being a genuine book production service. Even with a genuine book production service, book design is a separate task for which they will charge a fee and every fee you pay, adds to the production cost of your book.

Yes, I'm talking about saving money and every publisher does. If they have a hero, it's Scrooge in The Christmas Carol by Charles Dickens, or maybe Mr Macawber, well known for the adage: *"Annual income twenty pounds, annual expenditure nineteen pounds nineteen and six, result happiness. Annual income twenty pounds, annual expenditure twenty pounds nought and six, result misery."* (David Copperfield. Chapter 12)

The principle for success is worth repeating. If you intend to publish and sell a book, you are starting a business. Business is all about profit and loss, the product, or service is irrelevant. As the publisher, you should retain control over every aspect of production. Paying other people to undertake tasks you should and can do yourself reduces that level of control and also increasing cost. This is a very competitive market and the more you pay out, the more books you need to sell before you make a profit. The purpose of this book is not to make the process appear easy, but to help you do it right.

The benefit is that once you learn to do these things, you can apply this same knowledge to your next book, and the next.

Sizing a Book

The term to use is, Trim Size, the size of your finished book after it is bound and trimmed. For case bound books, the trim size is the size of the block of pages, called the book block, within the cover, the cover commonly extending beyond the trim size.

As a general rule, books are designed to a ratio of 2 to 3. A common size for case bound books is 6" x 9", complying to this ratio. Ie: (2x3)= 6". (3x3) = 9", a ratio of 2 to 3. Some larger paperbacks are also trimmed to this ration.

While this is a general rule, not all books comply exactly to this ration, but nor are they far out. For example, a common trimmed size for a paperback is 5" x 7¾", which is only ¼" out.

Books are these sizes for a number of reasons, the first being simply that this ratio is pleasing to the eye.

The second reason relates to methods of printing and the standard sizes on which books, magazines, journals et al are printed.

Pages are printed on sheets in multiples of four sides per sheet. These sheets are folded, bound and trimmed. Each page of a book is called a leaf. Each leaf has two sides, therefore two pages, recto and verso. When looking at an open book, the verso page is on the left, the even numbered pages, the recto is on the left, the odd numbered page, accept in countries where they read right to left, where recto and verso is reversed is reversed.

The finished size of a book is usually calculated as the width and height of the leaf, even with case bound books where the cover is commonly larger than the leaves inside. Historically, this measurement relates to the size of the leaf relative to the size of the sheet on which the leaf is printed. For example, the size quarto, was a book printed on a sheet of paper, folded twice to produce four leaves, eight pages, each leaf being one quarter of the size of the paper on which it was printed. The result is a range of standard book sizes with names relating to the number of leaves per sheet.

Folio = 12"x 9" folded twice.

Quarto = 9½"v 12" folded four times

Octavo = 6"x 9" - folded eight times.

12mo = 5"x 7"

16mo = 4"x 6¾"

18mo = 4"x 6½"

Down to 32mo and 64mo.

Just to complicate matters, depending on the type of press being used, a book with the finished size of 6"x 9 could be printed on sixteenmo paper, giving 16 leaves per side, 32 pages per sheet, folded 4 times giving an untrimmed size of by 6¼", but despite being folded 4 times, would still be viewed as an octavo.

Of course, as a publisher, you don't need to worry about the technicalities of this other than understanding that choosing a standard size for your book will reduce waste and therefore the price you pay to have your book printed. This is because printing cost is based on the sheets on which the book is printed so you will be paying for everything trimmed off and thrown away.

3. The third reason for sticking to standard dimensions is that bookshop shelves are designed to hold books of a standard size. Bookshop owners have more than enough reasons to not stock individual books by small publishers without offering one that won't fit on their

shelves.

Do not be afraid to discuss your plans with a printer before starting the design process. Printers do not expect you to understand he full technical details of their craft, but do appreciate you having a basic understanding and most are willing to offer advice and discuss the finished book sizes they prefer to work with. Note that these finished sizes do vary between different printers.

Note also that we are talking about the finished, trimmed size of your book.

D.T.P. Applications

You will here tell that you can format your book on your word processing application, or one of the new writing applications and technically, you can. Whether you should is another matter and virtually all printers can tell the difference and know that it is more likely for glitches to occur than when using an application designed for the purpose. The majority of modern book design is done using a DTP (Desk Top Publishing) application.

The main industry standard DTP applications are *Adobe In Design* and *Quark*. In Design probably has the greater technical capability of the two, but there are numerous versions and upgrades to consider when making this comparison. The drawback of this greater technical capability, in the opinion of some, is that In Design is more complicated to learn and use. Quark may have less technical capability, but can do everything required in book design. The fact is that both Adobe and Quark can do far more than is required to design a book, including maybe a few illustrations and a separate cover file. Many other lower cost DTP applications can achieve a similar quality output as that of these professional applications. Another benefit is that these smaller applications are easier to learn.

Consider for example and without making any recommendation, Swift Publisher and Print Shop for the Mac or Page Plus and Greenstreet Publisher for the P.C. These offer a suitable sub £80 ($100) alternative to the more expensive applications. Whichever you choose, the only requirement is that they are capable of producing PDF output. The rest is simply a matter of learning to use the application.

Most applications provide full instructions and a tutorial so what follows is for general guidance. Like any application, once you've used it a few times it becomes second nature.

The first step is to design a master page. Most DTP applications provide template designs that meet most standard requirements so it is only a matter of choosing your template design. If you want to do it yourself, the application gives you the opportunity to choose your chosen page size. You then select the size of your margins. More on this to follow. This is commonly done by setting a master page. The master page is the layout that future pages will follow, however, you will need to set up two master pages. With some applications it's four. One for the left hand page, called the verso, another for the right hand page is called the recto, and then one each for the reverse side of these pages. The screen view will allow you to see one page at a time, or two, the verso and recto, as if looking at an open book.

All DTP application work on the principle of boxes. This is similar to the text and picture boxes now available in Word and many other word processing applications. The difference is that you can't simply start typing, or upload a word processing file without first creating a box for the text, much as creating a text box in Word, except everything is done in boxes. Virtually all DTP application provide adequate instruction and guidance and it truly isn't that difficult.

Formatting for Print

The industry standard file form for this process is, Portable Document Format (PDF), so the DTP application you use must be capable of outputting a file in PDF format.

PDF is a standard, cross platform standard known as

ISO 32000 maintained by the International Organisation for standardisation. You don't need to know this, you do need to know that PDF files contain the complete formatting of the original document including text fonts and images enabling you to create a page layout that can then be read by the print-processing computer used by any printer.

There are also other things you need to decide; such as the page count you are aiming for. This can be increased or decreased by changing the font, the font size, line spacing, additions to the front or back matter, the space between chapter headers and first line of text, in fact a host of ways all related to design. Design is the process of getting it to look right and is an art form and a skill that takes time to acquire, but still not beyond the ability of the average individual.

Another question is, how many pages will fit on each signature. In litho printing, a multiple of four pages are printed on large sheets of paper. These are then folded into a signature prior to binding and trimming. The number of pages per sheet depends on the size of the sheet divided by the size of the page. This is commonly 16, 24, or 32 pages per sheet. Note: This is always a multiple of 4.

Knowing this, you can set the page count of your book, which should always be a multiple of the page count on each signature. For example: If there are 24 pages for each signature, the total page count should be 48 - 72 -

96 - 120 - 144 and so on. If there were 36 pages per signature, the total page count should be: 64 - 96 - 128 - 160 -224 and so on.

Designing a book with a page count that doesn't match the signature count creates addition waste. The printer won't mind because you're paying.

Paper

Uncoated, silk or gloss. White, Cream, Unbleached, Textured? The weight? Paper weight is measured in gsm (grams per metre), the higher the gsm the heavier the paper, but this does not necessarily relate to the thickness of each individual and therefore, the finished thickness of your book. You will need to know this to know the thickness of the spine when it comes to cover design. Paper thickness is measured in PPI, (pages per inch); so asking what the PPI of the chosen paper is will tell you the finished thickness of your book. Remember that there are two pages per sheet, recto and verso therefore the number of sheets will be half the number of pages. This total, calculated in PPI, will give you the thickness of your finished bookblock.

Novels, anthologies, poetry books and similar are usually printed on uncoated papers. A silk finish is usually reserved for photo and other specialist books. A gloss finish is also used for photo books and illustrated children's books or other books that contain a high volume of colour illustrations.

All printers have what they call *stock* papers, the paper they commonly use. These commonly range from 70 – 120 gsm uncoated and 115 – 170 gsm for gloss or silk finish. Using anything other than stock will likely increase printing costs. Most printers will also assist in the calculation of spine width.

Single Page/Spread Page

When opening a new file in any DTP application, you will be given a number of design options. One of the first is the choice between Single Page or Spread Editing Page layout. Single Page is as it says; you get one page at a time and all pages are the same. Spread Editing allows you to set up and view recto and verso pages on screen as well as individually setting the master bleed and gutter for recto and verso pages. To do this you need to go to 'Master Pages' and each application offers guidance on how to do this however, it does vary from application to application so I can't cover detail here, just the principles involved.

Design can be done in the Spread Page setting, but most printers will require the spread editing option to be switched off or deselected prior to outputting your final PDF file. While this should be a simple click of the mouse in the relevant option, the different lower cost DTP applications have certain idiosyncrasies; the reason they come at a lower cost. For example, if using spread editing in Apple iStudio publisher, there is no option to switch between spread editing and single page, though to allow for a gutter margin and other elements in recto verso page design, you need to format using the spread editing option. What happens is that when you create a PDF file there is a choice between Create PDF, which automatically creates a single page PDF, or Booklet PDF, which retains active spread editing in the file.

Choosing a Page Size

As covered at the start, books come in a range of standard sizes and once again, this is a marketing decision. Whether in a shop or at home, a book needs to fit on a bookshelf. These dimensions are called rack sizes, because this is a size that fits in point of sale bookracks that are designed to take a standard range of sizes. No shop is going to alter their shelf design for you so a book that doesn't fit, no matter how good the story may be, isn't welcome.

A book described as Mass Market will generally comply with the dimension circa 4¼" x 7".

Trade Paperbacks range in sizes between 5" x 7¾" to 6" x 9". A size of 5½" x 8½" is probably one of the most popular with shorter books tending to the smaller dimensions and longer to the larger 6" x 9" size.

The majority of case bound books measure 6" x 9", a size known as 'Royal' in the trade. Specialist books, children's picture books etc., add more options when selecting the dimensions for your book however, there are still some common standards and the individual printer will advise on those their system supports. You are the publisher. You decide, but consider the market when doing so.

As stated, the page size you choose will also affect printing costs. Choosing an odd size can lead to a lot of waste paper when folio sheets are folded and trimmed, all of which you pay for.

Note also that the range of page sizes available for full colour printing is usually more limited than that for mono printing.

Bleed

So far I've discussed choosing the final trimmed size of your book, but this is the final trimmed size and when you begin the design process and set the page size, there will be the option to add Bleed. Bleed is a margin in addition to the finished trim size, in effect, the bit that is trimmed away to give the correct finished trim size. Pages can be designed with or without Bleed, but if used, Bleed should be set at a minimum of ⅛" (circa 3mm) should be added to the outer three edges, not to the binding edge of the page.

Margins

In the world of book design, small things make a big difference. Book designers will pontificate about a layout change of millimetre, or hundredth of an inch and margins are not just the empty space running around the edge of the text. Margins are important. They allow the reader to hold the book without covering the text with their fingers. A margin that is too narrow can make the book appear less inviting to read whereas a good margin gives a feeling of openness. There is also the issue that when reading a book, the page is not flat, but curves towards the bound edge, so the inside margin includes the previously mentioned gutter margin. To look at, the inside margin is larger than the outside margin. The text is not centred on the page, though it appears to be because of the page being curved.

A common mistake with self-published books is to shrink the margin, to cram more words per page, thereby creating a book with fewer pages, making it cheaper to produce. BIG MISTAKE. Such books look self-published and those in the trade can read the genealogy of a book by its appearance.

Margins should be no smaller than ½" and up to ¾". Margins smaller than ½" can cause print smudging around the edges of the text during production. Top and bottom margins should be the same as the side margins, however, margins at the bottom of the page always appear larger because of the page numbering, commonly bottom centre of the page. The space between the bottom line of text and the page number should be the same as the margin between the page number and trimmed bottom of the page. As for the gutter margin, the additional margin that goes on the inside, binding edge of the page, this can be approximately ⅛"up to an additional ¼" maybe a little less.

When designing a book for the first time, it is a useful exercise to practice by creating a dummy book. Use any text to fill perhaps a dozen pages. Create a PDF file and then print them out just to see what they look like. Book design is a lot about achieving a book that looks right. Each page needs to look balanced and orderly. Which brings us to the subject of widows and orphans.

Take Note! If your margin is too small or narrow you may loose content when the finished book is trimmed. Variations of ⅛" can occur during the trimming process so all-critical content must be kept at least ¼" away from the final trim size. Offset print trimming is often more accurate than POD print trimming.

Gutter Margin

The Gutter is the area of the page taken up in binding process. The verso page is bound on the right edge, a recto page bound on the left edge. The size of the gutter margin depends on the binding method to be used. The purpose of the gutter margin is to ensure that the visible left and right margins of each page remain the same and that your finished book looks right and again, we're talking somewhere around ⅛" allowance as a Gutter margin.

Laying Out The Body

The body text of the book begins on a recto page after the front matter has been laid out. Recto pages are odd numbered pages; verso pages are even numbered pages. When looking at an open book, the recto page is on the right, the verso on the left, unless you are in one of the countries that read right to left, where this rule is reversed.

Ensure that you have linked text boxes, so that the imported text will flow from page to page. You will need this to occur while formatting your layout to the right look or adding illustrations. Different DTP applications have different methods of importing text and of creating linked text boxes. If you forget, text boxes can be linked simply enough during the layout process. It isn't difficult and the method will be described in the application instruction guide. Most also provide pre-created templates to get you going.

Page numbering commonly begins on the first page of the body text. The page numbering facility should allow you to set the page on which numbering is to begin and also what number that should be. For example, the front matter takes up six pages, that is, three verso/recto pairs. The body text therefore begins on page seven. Page numbering may start at page seven with the number 7. Alternatively, you may start numbered on page seven with the number 1. The only rule is that the body text starts on a recto page.

In some books the decision is made to start all chapters on a recto page though this is less common in modern book design as it can lead to blank verso pages and therefore waste of paper. That said, each new chapter should start on a new page whether verso or recto. Some layouts start a new chapter on the same page as the ending of the previous chapter, giving only a few lines between, but this generally looks untidy and lazy.

Kerning

Kerning is the ability to adjust the space between words and even individual letters. Print technology has moved on from the days of word block and hot metal, where letter spacing was measured in 'Em's. An Em is the size of the block used for the capital M that, when printed, could actually be slightly smaller than the block. Smaller letters such as the letter 'i' required smaller blocks, measured as a percentage of an Em. Modern print technology talks in *point* sizes, but the correspondence remains. For example, 1Em in a sixteen-point typeface equals the size of a capital letter M. The space between letters is important because it has to correspond to the size of the letter and those either side. If it did not, the text would look untidy and disjointed.

As stated, in word-processing this is done automatically, but in book design, especially where the text is justified to create even margins either size. The design application will adjust the kerning to allow this to happen, sometimes resulting in hyphenated words, which most designers try to avoid. But if they don't allow hyphenation, the line looks unnaturally spread out to create 'rivers' of white space between words. To resolve this, some DTP applications allow the designer to manually adjust kerning. However, not every DTP application has this facility but if yours does, this is what it is for.

Optical Margins

The ability to use optical margins is commonly only available with the more prestigious DTP applications. They only apply when using justified text, but the text layout in virtually all books is set to justified. The need occurs when a full stop, hyphen or other punctuation mark appears at the end of a line. Punctuation marks are small and less visible than any letter, yet they take up an equivalent amount of space. With justified text, the presence of a punctuation mark will force the more visible last letter of that line slightly in from the rest of the justified text. The use of optical margins allows punctuation marks to appear within the actual margin leaving all right hand line endings in perfect alignment.

Crop Marks

Some applications allow the facility to add crop marks. These mark the intended trim lines on each page, but most printers now prefer that they are not included in the final output PDF file. Confirm with the printer.

Using Illustrations

No illustration should be added to the word processing file prior to transfer. Illustrations are added to the DTP file separately, as it is being created.

The preferred graphic file format for all illustrations is TIFF (.tif) as this produces the highest quality with fewer technical problems, however, JPEG files are also acceptable.

Black and White (Mono) illustrations should be greyscale as this produces the best definition. Mono illustrations should be a minimum 800 dpi, up to 1200 dpi. Colour illustrations should be formatted to a minimum of 300 dpi, 400 dpi is most commonly used. Reproducing colour images as black and white may decrease quality. It is better to convert these to greyscale using a photo editing application prior to use.

Colour illustrations can be formatted using the CMYK system or use the Pantone Code (PMS or Print Matching System). CMYK stands for: cyan, magenta, yellow and black. Mixing these colours creates what in printing, is called, full colour. Your chosen printer should be able to give you more advice on this subject.

Note that the resolution quality of an image is related to the size at which it is reproduced. The maximum size for an image contained within a book is usually no more than 5"x 7", so a resolution of 300 dpi should be satisfactory. For a cover image that could be 6"x 9", the higher resolution of 400 dpi minimum would be required.

As a rough guide, the use of colour inside your book will increase the cost by up to 40%. The use of full colour on the cover does not increase the cost simply because is only involves one printing plate.

Widows and Orphans vs. Squared Off

In typesetting, widows and orphans are lines at the beginning or end of a paragraph that sit at the top or bottom of the page following or before the page containing the rest of that paragraph.

Depending on which manual of style is followed, an orphan is the first line of a paragraph, born and left alone, while the rest of the paragraph continues on the following page. A widow is the last line of a paragraph, left all alone with the rest of the paragraph on the previous page. Different editors and manuals of style disagree over which is which, some reversing the definition. However, the real issue is that widows and orphans make a page look untidy and there are various tricks that can be used to loose the untidy look created by widows and orphans.

Allowing or disallowing hyphenation is one. Disallowing a hyphenated word will force it onto the next line, pushing the text forward maybe enough to force the orphaned first line of a paragraph onto the next page. This may increase the kerning on that line, the space between words, but this may look better.

The traditional solution is to force an extra blank line at the bottom of a page. If the line is the first line of a paragraph that continues on the following page, then inserting a blank line forces it onto the following page re-joining it top the rest of the paragraph. If the line is the last line of a paragraph left alone at the top a page, inserting an extra blank before the last line on the preceding page will add another line to the top of the following page.

The problem is that the preceding recto verso pair will not be 'squared off'. Being squared off means that the text block on each pair of pages is the same, with the same number of lines, the same size border around each square of text. Forcing an extra line onto one page or the other means one page will have one line of text less than the other, not be squared off.

The solution you choose is one of personal preference. Put up with widows and orphans or put up with pages being not squared off. Personal I think widows and orphans are more obvious as these also interrupt the flow of reading a paragraph.

Creep

The issue of creep applies to all books where the pages are folded together and then bound. To illustrate creep, take ten A4 sheets, put them together and fold in half as if creating an A5 book. Put the pages together, in booklet form, as tight as you can and you will see that the edge of the inner pages, opposite the folded, binding edge, extend a fraction beyond the edge of the outer page. In fact, working in to the centre pages, the edge of each page extends a fraction beyond the edge of the next outside page. Therefore, working towards the centre, the block of text on each page will creep towards the outer edge and when trimmed square, the outer margin on each page working towards the centre, will be fractionally smaller.

The effect of creep on folded pages

The more technical of the DTP applications have the facility to set an allowance for creep, as do some printers. However, depending on the printing system being used, this doesn't apply to books that are to be perfect bound. Also, you should not need to worry too much so long as you're not using heavy grade paper, the heavier grade the paper the greater the measure of creep, or books made up a large size signatures, creep is something useful to know about, but not overly necessary to worry about.

Running Heads

A running head could be the author's name, the title, chapter title or other information that appears at the top of every page. You can choose to have running heads, or not have running heads. It is simply a question of personal preference.

The Cover

Designing the cover creates another set of choices. Case bound or paperback?

Case bound books are created using greyboard, approx. 2mm thick. This is covered with bookcloth or a usually colour printed laminate sheet. A dust jacket is optional for either finish.

For a paperback cover, the cover stock should be either 250gsm or 300gsm, commonly colour printed with either gloss or matte finish.

Whether case bound or softback, the choice between gloss or matte is a never ending argument. Gloss is considered more visually attractive and repels dirt, dust and can be wiped clean. The downside is that a gloss finish shows up scratches, creases and other marks more than a matte finish.

Matte finish is considered to be a softer, more natural look, less pretentious and in the opinion of some designers, a more professional look. The drawback is that the matte finish dulls the colour and is more likely to show stains and other dirty marks.

Most printers will supply a proof in both finishes allowing you to compare the two, but in the end, it is your choice.

The design of most covers includes a colour

illustration the same rules apply as for illustrations to go in the body of your book. The cover can be designed using a DTP or photo editing application, depending on personal preference. The cover design is often layered with different text boxes to contain the title, author name etc. and positioned where required. The application being used will supply instructions on how to do this.

The resolution of any colour image should be at least 300dpi, formatted as CMYK, 180 lines per inch with bleed. One place where bleed is important is in books where an illustration is designed to run to the edge of the page, as in some children's books. Another place is the cover because when did you last see a book cover with a margin? Once you have your design, this is again created as a separate PDF file. All books require two PDF files, one for the body of the book and one for the cover.

Now you need to think about the finish, whether the cover will be coated, uncoated, matte or gloss. The title can be embossed, or match etched, which is an image cut into the gloss coat covering the illustration. There are any number of interesting tricks that can be used to enliven your cover design and it is always better to discuss your ideas with a printer to be sure of their requirements before beginning the design process.

Remember that as publisher, these are your decisions and it is your responsibility to understand the process, even if you pay others to undertake the task.

Working With Printers

There are a few things to note when looking for a printer. The first and probably the most important is that it is not the printer's job to correct or even point out your formatting mistakes, or even discuss different options. That said, I have found that most printers are perfectly willing to discuss options and give advice if contacted prior to arriving with a readily formatted disk looking for a quote. What you are doing, in effect, is to dangle a potential job in front of them, as bait, and they will know that as a potential customer, you are more likely to use someone that is helpful than someone who is not.

Even so, the advice is to take three or four quotes before deciding.

And this is where advice will differ. Some will argue that it is better, and cheaper, to use one of the larger book printing companies because they will likely have presses set to print to a standard format. They will also have bindery equipment set to these standards as they are using them all the time while smaller printers, with less equipment, need to change the set up for each job. This set up time is what increases the cost.

It is a valid argument, but I have found small printers that are just as capable and able to match or even undercut these quotes simply because they have fewer or lower overheads.

One issue you will come across is that printers have a language of their own so a sample quote will give the title, the number of pages, the trim size, which are all very obvious. Then you might come across terms like: 1/1 on interior, and 60# natural. Then the print run followed by, cover 12pt c1s matte 4/1.

To explain these terms. 1/1 on interior, means 1 colour ink printed onto 1 colour paper. I.e., as most books are, black text on white or off white paper. 60# natural, or some variation, refers to weight and colour of the paper to be used.

When it comes to the cover, 12pt does not refer to the point size of the text but to the calliper measurement of the card to be used thickness. This is much more accurate than the gsm measurement of paper. 4/1 stands for four colour, or full colour printing and c1s matte stands for coated one side with matte varnish.

Of course there are any number of variations to these terms. The cover could be of a thicker paper. It could have a laminate finish. The book could contain internal illustrations. The above is just a guide to help you understand the process.

The printer will give you the option of digital or printed proofs. This is not an opportunity to correct any unseen spelling mistakes or change the content, but to ensure the printed page appears as you intended during formatting. Any changes, unless it is the printer's error, will cost you money. Printers work on a tight schedule so will expect the proof returned very quickly, most likely within 24 hours. Delay and your book can go to the back of the queue.

Select perhaps three or four printer and seek a quote from each. Compare not only their prices but also the quality of their work, reliability, and information from pervious customers. Now you are ready to go ahead.

E-PUBLISHING

E-publishing offers a number of advantages to the small independent publisher. The first of these is that it cuts out any reliance on the traditional marketing and distribution system. It negates the need to produce PDF files and doesn't involve the cost of physical book production. This in turn, is often dependent on volume production to achieve a reasonable per book retail price. The drawback is that anyone can produce an e-book and all those books are competition for the one you're trying to sell. This is a statement worth repeating.

Another disadvantage with e-publishing is that if you have a traditional book, you can go to fetes and book fairs and anywhere else you can get in and set up a table and sell the thing.

The biggest part of being a publisher involves recognising and understanding the market. Producing a book is the easy part. Anyone can do it because the main e-publishing suppliers provide the templates and instructions you need to publish using their system at no cost whatsoever. This raises the question of why some authors pay certain e-book publishing services to do this for them?

While e-publishing offers certain advantages, it also has some disadvantages and it is important that you recognise what these are. It is also important to recognise that publishing an e-book does not prevent you from also publishing a hard copy version.

E-Book Formats

With the rise of e-books came a whole host of different e-book formats such as, e-reader, formerly Palm, Fiction Book (Fb2), e-Book Apple, Mobi Pocket, Daisy (Digital Accessible Information System) specifically for those with disabilities, along with a host of independent and freeware e-reader applications.

Thankfully an increasing amount of cross-compatibility has left just two main formats to consider. These are the *Amazon Mobi* system and *e-Pub*, which covers Mobi, Nook, I-Pad, Sony and most android e-book systems. You can choose to publish your e-book in either Mobi, suitable for Amazon Kindle e-readers or e-Pub, for virtually every other e-reader system, though many of these are also capable of reading Kindle with the addition of a downloadable application that makes it possible. Alternatively you can publish your e-book in both formats, a Mobi version and an e-Pub version, along with a physical book version to ensure full coverage of the market. It is not a question of one or the other, but how to access whatever market there is for your book.

The Rules of E-book Publishing

This shouldn't need saying but it does. They are basically the same as for any book, but with a few succinct differences.

(1) The book has to be good.

(2) The cover should be designed to stand out against its rivals.

The difference with e-books is that the cover also needs to stand out when displayed as a thumbnail image. This creates a number of graphic design requirements, as this image must also comply with traditional book cover expectations.

(3) Price. The selling price remains an important issue despite the fact that being an e-book, negates the production cost of traditional books. Research shows that books priced between 99p -£1.99 (99 cents - $2.99) sell the most units while those in the £1.99 - £4.99 ($2.99 - $5.99) yield the most profit. Note that the comparison between British and American price does not conform to the exchange rate comparison. Publishers should therefore consider which market benchmark to use when setting their price.

Note also that some e-book platforms restrict the author's right to set the price and this brings us back to the issue of publisher identification.

The ISBN standard, ISO 2108:2005 states that: *"Each different format of an electronic publication (e.g. '.lit', '.pdf', '.html', '.pdb') that is published and made separately available shall be given a separate*

ISBN."

Most authors that publish using an e-book platform simply click the box for the e-book platform to supply the ISBN. This, as discussed previously, makes them the publisher and the publisher has the authority to set the price, despite what the author might wish. (Another issue that should be covered in the contract).

If you are going to remain the publisher and if you need to assign and register an ISBN to every separate e-book platform you publish under, along with another for a physical version, or even two (one for the case bound version, one for the paperback), then so be it.

(4) Marketing. There is no point in publishing a book if nobody knows its there and this applies to e-publishing in exactly the same way as to traditional book production. The main purpose of the ISBN system is to aid the identification of any publication so as to simplify market access. Now you need to remember that while e-book publishing is a simple process, it is a simple process that means anyone can do it and because anyone can do it, they do. This increases your competition so you will need to fight to get noticed.

Amazon Kindle Direct Publishing (KDP)

As with all e-publishing formats, your manuscript will need to be prepared ready to upload and many of the things said in previous chapters still apply.

The Amazon system provides directions on how to upload your manuscript file direct to KDP, thus avoiding the need to use any middleman who will take a cut of your profit.

Free software tools such as Mobipocket e-book Creator or Calibre allow you to create an e-book complete with a table of contents. This can then be converted into Amazon's AZW format.

Full information and a guide through the process is available on the Amazon Kindle website. It is important to note that Amazon's 70% royalty rate only applies to books priced above $2.99. Below that the rate is only 35%.

Smashwords

At the last count, Smashwords holds more than 125,000 titles from over 40,000 authors. These figures reveal that at least some authors are going back with a second and third book, unlike and as discussed, with some other 'we will publish your book' companies.

A Word file and cover image is uploaded into the Smashwords "Meatgrinder" tool. This allows the creation of an e-book in almost any format other than Kindle. Amazon has yet to update Kindle to automatically accept Smashword titles, though as discussed, your title can be published separately in both formats.

Smashwords offers a free style guide, available to

help you through the process, and with a bit of practice it is easy enough to produce a professional looking 'reflowable' e-book comparable to those produced by major publishers.

This 'reflowable' element is an important consideration because it allows the book to be read on a screen of any size.

Smashwords does take a small cut of author royalties, but offers the benefit of having your book made available on a wide range of e-publishing platforms. The books are available on Smashwords.com and can be distributed through, Barnes & Noble, Apple's iBooks, Sony, Kobo, Baker & Taylor's Blio and others.

Full information is available on their website along wit a free style guide to help you along.

Nook

From Barnes & Noble, this used to be called PUBIT and offers similar features to Amazon KDP, but there are differences in the process and royalty rates.

The PubIt system uses a conversion tool that takes a Microsoft Word, TXT, HTML, or RTF file and converts it to an EPUB file. This is then uploaded to the Barnes & Noble's e.Bookstore and the content previewed using a Nook emulator. Further information is available on the Barnes & Noble Pubit FAQ page.

Lulu

Lulu offers the option of publishing an e-book or P.O.D. or both. Lulu e-books are distributed through Lulu.com, Apple's iBookstore and the Barnes & Noble Nook. There is no charge for creating an e-book yourself using their e-book creator guide. A fee-based service is also available.

Booktango

Booktango comes from Author Solutions, one of the largest American self-publishing companies. Booktango offers a way to upload your manuscript, then edit to the correct format using WYSIWYG (What You See Is What You Get) common to D.T.P. Applications. Booktango seems to be a combined e-book generator and self-publishing application that in theory should offer a number of benefits, primarily the WYSIWYG ability to adjust page layout. The finished e-book can then be uploaded to Kindle, Nook, Kobo and iBooks as well as selling through Booktango. One benefit is that Booktango can roll e-sales from different formats into one single account.

Bookbaby

This is a system that allows you to sell your e-book on Kindle, Nook, the Sony Reader and I.pad. Instead of charging royalties, Bookbaby charges an up front fee of $99 followed by an annual charge of $19. per title held on their system. There are additional packages where they offer more help and assistance through the process, but there are additional charges depending on the level of help required.

iBooks Author

iBooks Author, from Apple moves into a field barely touched by other i-book systems. That is, books containing lots of images, such a children's books, nature and cookery books etc. There is also the ability to create touch and interactive books using a process similar to creating a PowerPoint presentation. The required programme is a free download to Mac users and books are available through the iBooks 2 application for i.Pad, i.Pod Touch and i.Phone. The programme includes templates to help you along the way with more available to download through third party vendors.

Other systems such as the Kindle Fire, the Nook Colour and Nook Tablet are becoming available meaning this is a developing field and like all good publishers, you need to remain aware of developing technology to keep up.

Scribd.com

Scribd allows you to create an account and then upload a PDF version of your manuscript. Their software then converts your book to a file that can be viewed on a PC, iPad and other portable devices. Unlike most other systems where the cover is a separate file, the cover picture needs to be embedded as the first page of this PDF book file.

One drawback is that Scribd is not a major player as far as e-book sales are concerned. The majority of documents, it might be wrong to call them books, are free to view or download. However, this does make this a simple way to post short stories and articles that might otherwise sit forgotten in a draw. This is a method of self-promotion that can help get you known so then and with a bit of luck, when you release your book on another platform, you will hopefully have a following that might be tempted to buy.

The would be e-publisher should note that this is not a recommendation for any of the above systems. It is the publisher's responsibility to research each and confirm whether the service they provide is suitable for your needs.

At present there is no legal deposit requirement applying to e-books. However, this is a subject under international inter-government discussion and a requirement may be introduced, at some time in the future that will require a copy of all e-books to be held on some central library mainframe system.

While e-reader ownership is a growing trend and

despite what some proponents of e-books are saying, it is unlikely that the e-book system will bring about the demise of physical books. In fact market research indicates that the advent of the e-book has led to an increase in sales of traditional books.

As a final point, the greatest problem is the belief that e-publishing brings automatic success. There are advantages and disadvantages. As the publisher, it is your task to select the best option for the style of book you are seeking to publish. One that is commensurate with your individual requirements and this is something only you, the publisher, can decide.

Print On Demand

I stated previously that the print-on-demand process resembles the system used by Vanity Publishers that resulted in the pulping clause common to some of their contracts and it does, according to the business model used by most printers. The general rule is, the higher the volume the lower the cost per item, despite the higher overall cost. This increased per book production cost limits the potential to sell books through bookshops and other outlets plus, bookshops do not buy one book at a time. An individual shop will purchase 10, or 20 copies, even more. A chain will purchase that number for each store, expecting a hefty discount for doing so, therefore negating the principle advantage of the print on demand process.

But the print-on-demand process does offer one main advantage. Books are printed in response to orders so negates the need for the author to pay a hefty up-front production cost.

The increased per book cost is countered by the fact that most print-on-demand titles are sold through a direct selling process and with adequate promotion, can result in reasonable success. Print on Demand is a perfectly viable way to produce and sell books, as long you are fully aware of the drawbacks as well as the advantages.

There is another major advantage I will come to but first, print-on-demand has its advantages but is also beloved by the vanity publisher. That said, there are also genuine POD services and probably the best known is Amazon's Create Space. Another is Ingram Spark and more on them in a minute.

There is a long-standing myth that bookstores will not stock books published on Create Space simply because they are published by Create Space. This is not true. The real reason is that under the expanded distribution system run by Create Space, a bookstore will only receive about 25% discount. As stated previously, the minimum most bookstores will accept on a fixed sale basis is 35%. This may be lowered, through negotiation, to 25% if you offer full sale or return, but Create Space don't do this.

Now we are back to the issue of the market. Some books will sell perfectly well on the print-on-demand direct sale system offered by Create Space. As a generalisation, I would list these as any non-fiction title or those with a specific target market genre. The market for general fiction has a different imperative, with a good portion being sold due to impulse buying, a person walking around a bookshop, liking the cover, liking the blurb and deciding then and there to buy. This impulse buying is more difficult to achieve when selling on a computer screen and part of the reason is simply, the potential customer doesn't get the feel of the book in their hand. More on this later, but one of the tricks in direct physical selling is to put the product, whatever it is, into the hand of the potential customer. Why do you think double-glazing salespeople carry a small sample window around with them? It's to get the product into the target customer's hand.

This is where companies like Ingram Spark might be a better alternative. Ingram is a mainstream book production company that produce and distribute for a number of mainstream publishers. Ingram Spark is a subsidiary that specialises in short run book production for independent small press publishers. They also provide an e-book service.

Note the term, *short run book printing*. This uses the same digital book production processes as print-on-demand, but counters the cost of printing one book at a time, in response to orders, by printing in small batches of maybe 100, or 50, or even 25.

More importantly, Ingram Spark will allow bookstores up to a 40% discount, not that this guarantees your book will appear on a bookstore shelf, but at least it becomes a possibility.

The drawback is that as the author, the percentage royalty you receive is less with Ingram Spark than with Create Space, therefore you will need to sell more books to break even, but getting your book onto the shelf of any bookstore will give you the opportunity to sell more books and all of this is for the publisher to decide. Weigh the advantages against the disadvantages and decide.

Note that this is not a recommendation for using Create Space, or for using Ingram Spark and there are other POD companies, for example, BookPrinting UK, that offer a comparable service. Again, this is not a recommendation to use any of these services.

As an exercise, during the research for this book, I sought quotes for the production of a standard paperback novel from a number of short run book production companies and from another that I consider to be a vanity publisher. From those I view as genuine short run production companies, the per copy price for print runs of 25, 50 and 100 were fairly close, along with the recommendation that a print run of 25 was the minimum viable due to increasing set up costs. The price for 100 copies, printed from supplied PDF files, bound and delivered, all came in circa the £400.00-£440.00 mark. For the same book, the vanity publisher quoted £1,436.00, for which I would receive 5 copies, the remainder printed on demand at an additional per book fee.

However, from the perspective of selling through the book trade, a production cost of over £4.00 per book leaves too little margin when compared to the average retail price of many mass-produced books. It's all about the market and knowing the viable selling price for the book you intend to publish compared to the total cost of producing that book and bringing it to the market.

Printing on demand, or short run production can be viable and your task, as publisher, is to ensure that whatever production method you use, the margins are there to enable the book to be sold at a profit.

And this brings us to another advantage of the digital book production methods that enable short run production and print on demand.

D.I.Y.-P.O.D.

Print-On-Demand is made possible by the advent of digital production methods and the subsequent improvement and development across the various different elements of book production.

Home printing has developed from the clattering of the dot matrix printer. Low volume reproduction systems such as the duplicator and photocopier have also, to an extent, been replaced by the inkjet and laser printer. The output quality of these printers has also improved to virtually equal that of litho printing.

The POD system uses a digital print process. However, your average home desktop inkjet or laser printer is a digital printer. The printers used in professional short run production might be larger, bulkier and run at a higher speed, but are basically the same beast, a digital printer.

You could, if you wanted, print your book on the cheapest ink jet printer you could buy. Not that I would recommend you do this, but it would still be digital printing.

The key difference between inkjet and laser printers is that with inkjet printers, depending on the type of ink, most inks soak into the paper. With a laser printer, the ink lays on top of the paper without soaking in. This reduces the chance of soak through and gives a better appearance.

Print quality is measured in dpi (dots per inch), the common target being 400dpi, a figure easily within the reach of the average home laser printer and it would take a professional to spot any difference. It is therefore entirely feasible to print, once the layout and design are done, the body text of own book.

We will now look at the D.I.Y. process in detail

Printing

As stated previously, you can use an inkjet printer but a laser printer will give better quality output. To simplify the task, you will want a laser printer with automatic duplex facility. This means the printer automatically prints both sides of the paper.

I recommend avoiding low cost printers. A larger, professional/office quality laser might cost more to purchase, but the per page printing cost can be more than halved. As a rule, printers that take a larger toner drum are cheaper to run than the small home printer, something to always keep in mind.

Colour laser printers tend to be more expensive to run and should only be purchased if there is a specific need. Mono laser printers cost less to run and considering the content of most books is text, a mono laser will be sufficient for most tasks.

You will need a printer with automatic duplex facility. This is the ability to print on both sides of the paper without needing to turn the pages over and reinsert in the paper tray before printing the second side. In short, you will need a professional/office quality mono duplex laser with the ability to print at least 400 dpi.

Print from the PDF file, not from the DTP Application file.

When printing a PDF, the computer will likely open *Acrobat Reader*. Simply follow the print dialogue directions. One of these is the *Print Booklet* option. With some older applications, you will first need to use the option, *Create Booklet*. With the booklet option and printing on A4 paper, and sub A5 page size will automatically be formatted to print starting with the first and last pages on opposing sides of the A4 sheet with the centre pages printed last. All that needs doing then is for the A4 block to be cut in half and the two halves placed together to form an A5 size book-block.

Ensure you select the print both sides option. You will be asked whether you want long edge or short edge binding. Most books are bound on the long edge and despite that you are printing on A4 paper the finished pages for a standard book will be laid out for long edge binding.

I mention this because different printers react differently to this instruction and if set wrong, will invert the print on the verso page. If your printed page comes out with one page inverted, changing this long edge/short edge option should resolve the issue.

For printing larger page sizes, for example, for a 6"x 9" finished size, do not use the booklet option, remembering that you will only get 2 pages per A4 sheet so increasing the paper cost. However, one of the benefits of working with PDF is the option to scale the finished product. You can, for example, design your book with a finished page size of 6"x 9" and use this same PDF to print as a booklet, remembering that the finished text and everything on the pages will be automatically scaled down to fit. Note also that this automation creates another issue when printing a booklet. This layout will also be scaled down to allow for the printer's boarder settings when setting up to print a booklet. This is only a fraction decrease but can be avoided by selecting the paper as A4 borderless.

Most issues are minor and can be resolved with a little bit of experience and practice, but the simple fact remains, you can print the body text of your own book.

One issue you may come across in doing your own printing is that you will be limited to printing on A4 paper and this can result in the two sides of the printed pages not being correctly aligned. There are several fixes for this problem, manual adjustment of the printer settings, altering the paper size while still printing on

A4, clicking centre page, though this will result in the need to trim the binding edge prior to binding. A far simpler solution is to design the book layout with this issue in mind.

For example: To create a paperback book with a finished size of 5" x 8", but setting the page size to A5, to simplify self printing, set the left hand, binding margin to ¾", the outside margin to 1½". Also, set the top and bottom margins to 1½". These margins are the distance between the edge of the A5 page and the printed text. When trimmed to the finished 5" x 8" size this will leave a margin of circa ½" between the text and edge of the page. Remember to allow for the position of the page numbers.

When using this method there is no need to worry about gutter margins and the rest and with practice, you can calculate the margin requirements for any size book you wish to produce despite being limited to printing on A4 paper.

The Cover

The cover needs to be printed on at least 200-gsm card. 300-gsm card is better.

GSM is a measure of paperweight and most desktop quality lasers don't like anything above 200-gsm. You can print your own covers using an inkjet printer, but most inkjet inks fade in sunlight and the finished quality can fall short of the ideal. One of the new solid ink printers is another option, as the ink resists fading better than the ink used inkjet printers. A colour laser is also an option, but a big expense for just printing covers and perhaps only justified if you plan to print books colour illustrations, such as books or children. The bigger problem is the limitation of page size to A4 which, when allowing for the spine, isn't even large enough to print a cover for a book with a finished size of A5. To allow for the spine, such books are commonly printed on B4 or A4 paper and then trimmed to size. Despite this limitation, A4 is large enough to print on for the cover of an average paperback of about 500 pages.

The most viable option is to take your PDF cover file to a printer and get the covers professionally printed. Your cover is, after all, the first and best visual selling point for you book. A small error inside can be overlooked, but the cover needs to be right. For your cover you have two options.

Case bound covers usually consist of two pieces of card called grey board or binder's board, for the front and back, plus another, thinner piece for the spine. A space of about ⅛" - ¼" is left between the back and front boards and the spine, called the joint, to allow the book to open freely. These boards are covered and held together by, leather, book cloth or printed paper, in fact anything you wish, cut to a size large enough to wrap around the whole book plus to overlap the inner edge of the cover. The spine is strengthened using a liner and super with an added headband top and bottom. Unlike perfect binding, the spine of the bookblock is not attached to the cover. The bookblock is attached to the cover using endpapers, fastened to the first and last pages of the bookblock and to the inside of the cover. Case bound books normally have an added dust jacket, so called because its original purpose was to protect the cover from gathering dust, but are now printed and illustrated as a primary marketing tool, the actual cover sometimes left blank or with gold blocked title and author name on the spine. This gold blocking is not required if the cover is made using printed paper, but a matching dust jacket will add a little status to the look of the finished book.

Making your own case bound covers can be considered more a craft enterprise than a viable business option, however, considering that the average per copy book sales for self published books is well below 100 copies and that case bound books demand a higher retail price than the paperback version so it might be worthwhile considering.

One issue with case bound books is that traditionally, the pages of each signature are stitched together, requiring specialist machinery, but some short run print companies now glue bind the body of the book in a paper wrap. This is then glued into a traditionally designed case, giving a case bound book that some purists might deride, but it does work. Even so and even with modern machinery, case making remains a more labour intensive task than paperback production. If you want to have a go, there are books on bookbinding that illustrate the whole process from start to finish.

When designing your cover, you will need to get the position of any illustrations used correct, along with the position of the title, author name, spine width, back blurb, ISBN number, will all need to be calculated and the way to confirm these calculations are correct is to create a dummy.

In the chapter on book design I described how spine width is calculated according to a paper's ppi (pages per inch). The more modern alternative is to search *spine width calculator* online. Enter the number of pages, select the paper type and note the result. Even so, a purist will use this measurement to create a dummy just to ensure perfection.

A dummy is a mock up of your book. It is a bookblock made up of however many pages there are, often blank, but you can print a draft copy to check the internal layout at the same time as designing the cover. Now print your cover, fold and crease. Put in place, check all the dimensions. When you think you've got it right, bind and trim for a final check.

Your cover will also need to display an ISBN barcode and you can purchase the ISBN barcode creation application from the ISBN Agency. Note that ISBN barcodes are different from standard shop barcodes, so while using a standard barcode application will result in a barcode image, this will not correspond to the correct ISBN barcode image. The barcode image commonly goes in the bottom right hand of the rear cover. Create the barcode, save as a TIFF image file, and then import this to the cover design.

With the cover designed and tested for size, by creating a dummy of your book, export as PDF, copy the file to a disc, go along to a printer, get a price, get a proof. Go back and check this fits. Tell the printer how many you need printed and on what stock, glossy, semi-glossy, laminated. You're the publisher so you decide and most printers are only too happy to give advice if you ask. After all, they will be hoping you come back with further business.

Now you have your covers and you can print the body of the book as required leaving print finishing as the final task, or list of tasks.

Folding and Creasing

The requirement to pre-fold and crease your cover depends on the binding method being used. Some of the more expensive desktop thermal perfect binding machines do this as an all in one process while some of the low cost hot glue binders are little more than a heating element set in a frame.

Pad binding is another method where you may need

to pre-crease the spine width of your cover and more on this in a minute. Whether you need to pre-crease your covers before binding will become clear after the next section. If so, ranges of different manual creasing machines are available for purchase through a number of different suppliers.

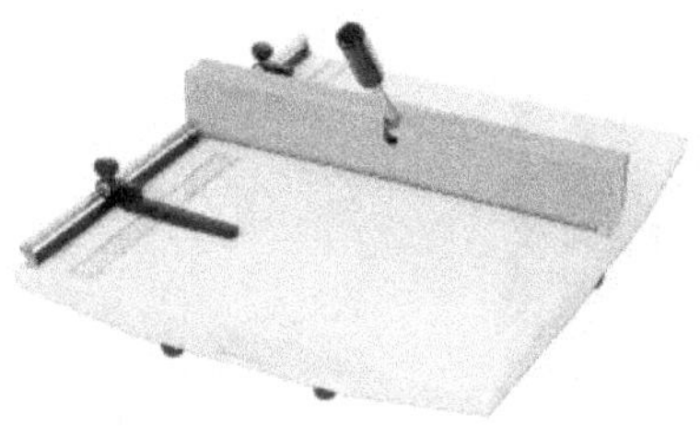

A small desktop creasing machine

Perfect Binding

In Perfect Binding the pages are simply glued into a card cover. The finished glued book is then trimmed to size.

Modern perfect binding commonly uses hot melt glue, though the previous method, known as pad binding, remains a viable alternative. In pad binding a stack of bookblocks are placed together in a padding press. This is simply a clamp to hold and squeeze the pages in place while being glued. A non-acid glue must be used, commonly PVA. Special padding glues are also available, some called non-permanent, for things like drawing pads, post it pads and the like. Non-permanent refers to where the pages are to be separated later on. For books, always use *permanent* padding glue.

In padding, the books are stacked and pressed together using a padding press. Glue is then brushed onto the spines and allowed to dry. Another method is to apply a first coat of PVA mixed 50/50 with water. This allows the glue to soak a little further into the edge of the paper, to strengthen the gluing effect. This is allowed to dry and then a second, full strength coat of PVA is applied. When dry and released from the padding press, each individual bookblock is separated from the stack using a padding knife. Another coating of glue is applied to the spine to glue the bookblock in the cover and allowed to dry.

A common type of padding press

There are various different methods of thermal hot glue binding and a range of different binding machines. The most basic of these is simply a frame to hold the book with a heating element to melt a strip of hot melt glue that is pre-applied to the spine. The suppliers of these machines can also supply printed covers to your own design with the glue applied, though these tend to be expensive. An alternative is to fold and crease your cover and then apply an even layer of hot melt glue to the inside of the spine using a holt melt glue gun. Put the cover into the binder, add the book block, following the timing and other instructions that come with the binder.

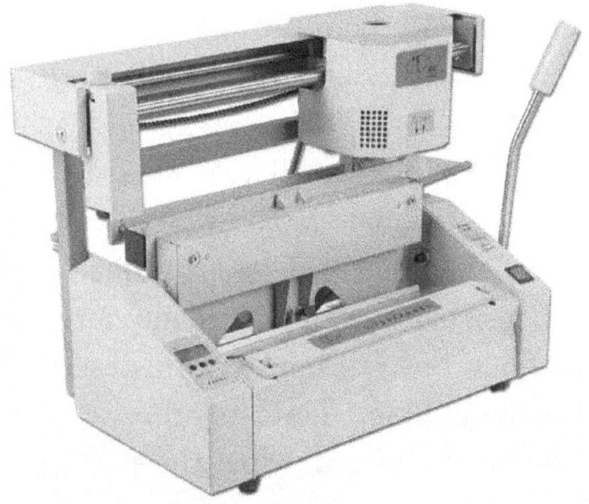

A desktop hot glue binding machine

Note that this is a manual and low cost method that requires practice to achieve satisfactory results.

For professional results it is better to invest in one of the automated tabletop perfect binding machines and here you may come across a technicality in their description. In searching on-line, those described as thermal binding machines tend to be at the lower cost, more basic range. Those described as perfect binding machines range from the desk-top size to the larger industrial machines used by short run printers. In the desk-top range of perfect binding machines, these range from the more manual machine to the almost fully automated. With these the book-block is placed in clamp and the cover inserted, ensuring it is the correct way round. The machine automatically applies glue, from a reservoir of melted hot glue granules and wraps the cover around the book block, folding and creasing as it does so. Some models can bind up to 90 books an hour.

All these machines are relatively easy to use and can produce professional looking results, the prime difference being that the less automated machines produce books at a slower rate. Some can even be used with case bound covers, but trying to describe their use is close to impossible. There are however, a number of videos on YouTube showing the varying kind of machine in operation. Just go to YouTube and search, desktop perfect binding machines.

Trimming

Your printed and bound books now need trimming to size and despite being made of paper and card, cutting through even 50 sheets requires the use of a tool designed for the purpose.

The options are, go to your local print shop and pay them to trim your books. A small local print shop will be more willing to do this than a larger organisation.

Manual ream cutter on optional stand.

Purchase a ream cutter, which is as the name indicates, is a manual guillotine designed to cut up to a ream (500 sheets) of paper at a time.

Purchase an electric guillotine. Small, relatively simple to use machines are available, but second hand machines are also available, many at a fraction of the cost of new machines.

Trim the top, bottom and outside edge of your book. You will also need a guillotine to cut your printed A4 bookblock in half. Put the two halves together ready to bind.

Of course many of these tools are not the sorts of thing that you want in your front room, but it is perfectly possible to set up your own little bindery in a garage or garden shed. And yes, doing this involves an initial investment in the equipment required. However, these tools, especially things like guillotines etc., can be found second hand on places like Ebay or specialist second hand print equipment suppliers. Then there's the learning process, but it's not that difficult. The benefit is that once you have the equipment, you can produce as many books as you require without needing to pay someone else. You can also, as I have done, go on to produce short print run books for other people, not that I want to do too much of that or even produce your book for you. I'm a writer at heart.

So there is an up-front cost for the equipment you will need, but how much will you have to pay someone else to publish your book and how much will they need paying to produce a second print run, or a second book. Do it yourself and all you will need to pay for are the materials required.

A LITTLE BIT OF BUREAUCRACY

So you've written, edited, formatted and produced and set the launch date for your finished book. You've also registered your book with the relevant ISBN agency. For books published in the UK its Nielsen and books can be registered as being published online at the Nielsen Bookdata website http://www.nielsenbookdata.com/pubweb. For books published in other countries, the relevant ISBN agency there will provide full information and all the relevant links.

Books can be registered prior to the date of publication, as long as you know when the book will be available for sale. Once registered, the book is listed on a central database of books in print. Major distributors, bookstore chains, Amazon etc., all have their own database and all of these automatically scan the ISBN database for new books in print and transfer these details across. You don't need to do a thing. Any publishing service provider that makes a big deal of making sure your book is listed on Amazon and every major bookstore chain is claiming credit for something that happens without them doing anything more than registering your book with the relevant ISBN agency.

Doing this also allows for pre-publication marketing promotion and even sales orders.

Another task is to comply with all Legal Deposit

requirements and as the name states, in the U.K. it is a legal requirement based on the Legal Deposit Libraries Act 2003 and the Copyright and Related Act 2000. This states that it is the publisher's responsibility to deposit, within 1 month of the date of publication, one copy of your book with the British Library.

The address for this is:

> The Legal Deposit Office
> The British Library.
> Boston Spa
> Wetherby
> West Yorkshire
> LS23 7BY

Sometime after this you will receive a request, from the Agency for the Legal Deposit Libraries, for further 5 copies, one copy to be deposited at each of the following. The Bodleian Library, Oxford University - The Cambridge University Library - The National Library of Scotland - The National Library of Wales and Trinity College Dublin.

This is also in accordance with the Legal Deposit Libraries act 2003 and comes in a nice letter stating, 'I would like to request,' however it is a legal requirement to send these copies at your own expense.

The address for the Legal Deposit Office is:

(ALDL) at the Causeway Building,
161 Causewayside,
Edinburgh
EH9 1PH.

Contact www.legaldeposit.org.uk for further information.

Books published in the United States come under the regulation of Mandatory Deposit (17 U.S.C. section 407). This requires the owner of copyright, or of the exclusive right of distribution, to deposit in the U.S. Copyright Office for the use of the Library of Congress two complete copies of the best edition within 3 months of the date of first publication. (*See* Copyright Office Circular 7d, *Mandatory Deposit of Copies or Phonorecords for the Library of Congress,* and the Deposit Regulation 202.19).

Note that there is a difference between mandatory deposit and copyright registration. Section 408 of the copyright law provides the option to formally register the work with the U.S. Copyright Office. This registration process provides a legal record of copyright ownership as well as additional legal benefits in cases of infringement. While copyright registration comes at a cost, it does fulfil mandatory deposit requirements, but without copyright registration, the publisher is still subject to the mandatory deposit requirement. Mandatory deposit copies should be sent to:

Library of Congress
Copyright Office-CAD 07
101 Independence Avenue, SE
Washington, DC 20559-6607

Foreign publishers should note that they also become subject to the deposit requirements of the United States if they import and distribute an American edition of any work first published in a foreign country. In such a case, the deposit requirement is one copy.

This completes the bureaucratic requirements involved in publishing a book.

MARKETING & PROMOTION

Promoting Self

The rule in marketing is, if you don't blow your own trumpet, nobody else is going to do it for you. Then you need to blow it loud enough and hope others take up the tune.

The Internet makes this appear a far easier task than once it was, leading to the expectation that you need to do is have an author website, or rely on the likes of Facebook and Twitter, maybe do a bit of blogging, or join various author sites and the rest will follow.

Blogging gives you the opportunity to display to the public that you can write. The comments you receive when involving yourself in discussions on various author sites can show that you know what you are talking about, or not, whatever the case may be. However, any reliance on the Internet, believing that simply putting information about your book out there, in the ether, will bring results, is a mistake made by far too many self-publishing authors. The simple fact is that it is easy to do and because it is easy, everyone is doing it. And from a marketing perspective, this increases the competition. The result is that there is a lot of the information out there, floating around in the ether that is rarely ever seen.

Remember that even famous people spend a lot of time on self-promotion. Whenever there's a new play, film, record being released, the stars do the rounds, appearing on quiz shows and chat shows, in fact anywhere they can get a foot in to publicise their latest whatever it is.

You face the problem that you're not famous. You're not even well known, so you're not going to be invited on some T.V. chat show or similar. You'll even struggle to get on local radio or television, or to even get an item in the local press, unless you have an angle.

An angle is something that makes the fact that you have just published a book newsworthy.

Never forget that the local press measure their content in column inches and each inch has a cost. Any item they publish needs to be newsworthy enough to justify the cost. Radio and television measure the cost of any item they transmit in seconds. The fact that you've just published a book is not news. The fact that recently, someone with dyslexia just wrote and published a book gave the story enough of an edge to earn itself a small new slot on local television. You need an edge.

Now a look at some methods to promote your book other than the infernal net.

The Advance Information Sheet.

An advance information (AI) sheet is probably the first

tool to be used in the bookseller's arsenal and is mainly sent by the publisher to wholesalers and booksellers. Major wholesalers include information provided by this method in the catalogues they produce, but don't count on this as a guarantee of sales. These catalogues contain vast quantities of information and that is all, but they do supply booksellers with the information needed to fulfil customer requests for a book they do not stock.

Note that most of these catalogues are now on-line and this information is also available through the ISBN system.

An AI sheet does not need to go into details of plot, characters or anything about the story. The only things any retailer wants to know is whether the book will sell, the title, how much and where to order from.

An AI sheet is sent to wholesalers, the central stock buyer for the retail chains and library suppliers. This should be done at least two or three months before the book's publication release date; there's no point sending this out after publication.

The Press Release.

The target of a press release is the media, newspapers, magazines, radio, and television and should be no more than a single side of A4 paper.

A press release is a news item so, in effect, you are trying to sell them a news item that, as stated above, will cost them time, or column inches. The people you are targeting are also all very busy. They don't have the time and more importantly, won't make the time to faff around trying to work out what you mean. You need to be clear and concise, straight to the point and use as few words as possible, 200 words maximum and some will say this is too many.

People say that writing a press release is even harder than writing a synopsis, and not a joke. Hiring a professional publicist, who does this sort of thing all the time, can be expensive with no guarantee that even they will get it right.

Then there is also the issue of luck. On a slow news day even a poorly written press release might get picked up, but if a major disaster occurs at the same time as your press release lands on the editor's desk, it'll go straight in the bin.

Even when using one of the many book production services and the additional marketing and promotion services they provide, don't simply leave it to them. You need to check the quality of what they are doing. Ask to see a sample of any press release they send out and if you don't like it, ask if you can write your own. Ask for a list of the publications they say they are going to contact and ensure the contact is not just by e-mail. These tend to get junked without being read.

Nor should you wait until the book is published before sending a press release, but by then it will be old news.

Nor can you send it too long before the publication date, because it won't yet be news. However, you need to give the various aspects to the media you contact time to respond. If you are lucky, the first contact will probably be a phone call seeking further information or seeking to arrange an interview. If you are having a book launch, and you should, this of itself is a potentially newsworthy event. If so, be sure to add the date time and venue to your press release.

To start, put PRESS RELEASE in big capitols at the top of the sheet, repeated across the top if you want.

You will then want something that grabs the attention. Avoid words like *dramatic* and other adjectives because you're dealing with professional writers and all adjectives are padding.

This is newsworthy because... is what they want to know and what you need to tell them.

Add any relevant information such as local interest, local setting, anything that makes the story more newsworthy. Add a picture of the cover and do not forget to quote the ISBN number and your contact details, name, address, phone number, email. This has happened.

While the idea of authors publishing their own books is becoming more and more acceptable, the term self-publishing continues to face a certain level of discrimination, from some quarters more than others. But this doesn't apply because you will have done it properly and the phrase: 'the first title by new independent local publishing company,' is of itself a potentially newsworthy story.

What you should NOT do when constructing a press release is use a catch all approach. Local newspapers have different requirements to national newspapers. Different magazines require a different angle of approach. Radio and television are different again. Adapt the information in your press release to suit the target and accept the principle that you will have more luck with the local and regional than with national media, but you never know where Lady Luck may strike.

The Book Launch

The days of the big brash stylebook launch are, for the most part, something that no longer happens. However, it remains true that more business is done at the bar or in a restaurant than in the office, the person paying being the one that wants something, but there is always a quid-pro-quo. The grand book launch was just another such venue, held to promote other business as much as the book is being launched.

The modern book launch is generally a more subdued affair but whatever the size, the rule to apply is that it needs to be worth the effort. This means understanding that the whole purpose is to gain publicity that will eventually result in extra sales.

Referring back to the press release. A press release announcing your books publication is one thing. A press release announcing your books publication along with a book launch is another. It doesn't need to be big and brash. A small buffet and a few bottles of plonk will do, as long as you can entice enough people to attend. If you are a regular at a local bar or pub, the landlord will likely give you a good deal because of the extra drinks they'll sell. Other venues can be hired, but always consider the cost. Consider that on one hand, holding a book launch is an investment you hope will pay off in future sales. On the other hand, it is also a business expense, the cost of which can be laid off against the tax you will have to pay on the profit made from selling all those extra books.

Invite family and friends. Send invitations to the local press, radio and television. You'll need to be famous to gain national interest, but there's no harm in trying. If you belong to a local writing group or the like, there's another obvious group to invite. Then think outside the box, to people who are always vying to get a share of any publicity going, such as your local councillor, even your local M.P. Give them plenty of advance warning because they are busy and be sure to tell them you've invited the local press, radio and television. Then tell the local press, radio and television that you've invited your local councillor and M.P etc.

Alternatively, combine a book launch with a book signing. Most bookstores are now part of some multinational chain, but most managers are still permitted a certain level of autonomy when it comes to local promotions and publicity. Make an appointment and simply ask if you can hold a combined book launch and book signing, for which you will be sending out a press release and arranging other publicity. What you are doing is offering them free publicity and all businesses like free publicity. They like anything that encourages customers to enter their store. They don't even need to stock your book. You will bring these along and any sold will go through the shop's till, with them taking their cut, but that's fair enough.

Offer to provide a poster for their window and if they agree, be sure to make it look professional. Ask if they can provide a table and chair. Most will but never take anything for granted. Then turn up with more than one pen. They do run out and if you can't sign your own book, what's the point? In short, make sure you are properly organised. And be sure to have someone there to take photos, just in case the press don't turn up. Proper photos, better than taken on most mobile phones. Just because the press didn't turn up doesn't mean you can't have another shot at sending another press release, along with a photo, preferably showing a crowd around your table, announcing that you held a successful book launch.

'Crowds flock to launch of new book by local author at ....' and so on.

Book Signings

Some will argue that a book signing is a different event from a book launch, but as I've shown above, for a small independent publisher, combining the two may be the most cost effective and beneficial option; from a seeking publicity standpoint.

Book signings are commonly held in a bookshop and as above, most managers are granted a certain level of autonomy in arranging such things. But bookshops are not the only venue where you can hold a book-signing event. In fact I wouldn't reject any potential venue, though in some cases this will depend on the type of book. Non-fiction is easy. If it's a book on swimming, consider holding a book-signing event at your local lido. If it's a book on steam railways, hold one at one of the preserved railways doted around the country.

Fiction is another matter when it comes to such specialised venues, but supermarkets sell books. So do a lot of other places. Don't think that a book signing can only be held in a bookshop. There are fetes and fairs where you can rent a table. Make a freestanding sign announcing why you're there. String up some balloons, anything to draw people over. There's more on how to do this in the next chapter, but there is nothing to stop you holding a book-signing event anywhere.

Now, I stated that you want a table and chair, but don't just sit there and expect people to come to you. In fact, don't sit down at all. Stand up so that you can meet people's eyes as they glance your way, which they will. Catch their eye, then smile. That will hold their glance for another second or so. Don't waste it. Walk up to them. Say, hello and ask them a question. It can be a leading question or an innocuous question, anything to get them talking. Then introduce the subject of why you are there. Again, more on this in the following chapter.

The Hype

Hyping up a book is a particular form of hard marketing in which it seems impossible to escape from hearing about the book wherever you go. In addition to the usual general advertising, the book is mentioned on chat shows, news programmes and commonly accompanied by words like phenomenon.

One such recent series of books given the hype treatment sold millions however, a week later copies began turning up in second hand shops, car boot sales and charity shops. One charity chain received so many donations of this book that they refused to accept any more and by their condition, most people had read more than the first few chapters.

Another form of hype is with a book who's content can be viewed as controversial. A copy of a book with content that could be described as risqué/erotic/pornographic, depending on you point of view, was sent to a well-known anti-porn campaigner with a letter purporting to be *Disgusted of Chelmsford* or something similar, demanding that something should be done. The book received so much free publicity that it sold far more copies than justified by the quality of its content. And this is not the only case where this has happened. Controversy sells! Not that I advocate this type of marketing and promotion, claiming the information is here only to be completely informative.

And The Rest

One of the reasons major publishers are reticent to take on new authors is because of the cost involved in promoting that new author and their new book to a level that will achieve the sales return they need to see a profit on their investment. In fact the first edition of a new book by a new author commonly doesn't show a profit at all. It's the nature of business and business is all about cost and profit, though publishers are willing to play the long game. The first book breaks the ice, the second and third reap the dividend. So publishers like to be sure that any author they publish is more than a one trick pony.

The small publisher benefits from lower overheads and can achieve success with a lower sales target than a major publisher, but the cost of promotion is just another cost to be added against the profit margin of your book. Businesses have gone bust because they've paid out too much on advertising, so here is a warning.

But first, a true story.

A friend of mine, who runs a small business, came in boasting about the latest advertising project he'd just been sold. A sign advertising his business would appear over the counter in nearly every post office in the region, for what he claimed was a very minimal cost. Seeing that I wasn't impressed, he asked why. So I asked him to describe the sort of people that commonly use a post office. His answer was pensioners, people posting letters and so on. Then I asked him what his business was and who his customers were. Then he twigged that his customers weren't the sort of people that commonly used the local post office. Of course they might, occasionally, just as anyone might, but not enough to justify the cost of advertising in that location.

The point is that the people who sell advertising space are there to sell advertising space. It's not their job to worry about whether that advertising space is beneficial to you, or your business, or the book you are trying to sell. That is your job. Their job is to sell advertising space, nothing more.

So, there are countless blogging sites, websites, and other services that advertise ways to promote your book and any attempt to list the various options would go on forever, but the task of the people promoting and selling space on these various sites is to sell space on these sites and it is all too easy to fall for glib advertising spiels that sound good but deliver little in the way of results.

It is down to you to compare the cost of advertising and promotion against the return in increased sales. If £100 of advertising brings a £75 return in increased sales, you are still loosing.

Marketing and promotion is often seen as a necessity, but the real necessity is the ability to sell the book you've just published.

THE PRINCIPLES OF SELLING

When it comes to selling, marketing and promotion is just fairy dust. You can market a book to kingdom come and not sell a single copy, but you can sell a numerous quantity without a single ounce of marketing or promotion.

Some marketing people will argue that selling is part of marketing as a whole and it is, in a way, but in the same way that closing a sale is part of selling. If you can't close a sale, there is no point doing the introduction and presentation. If you can't sell, there is no point in doing the marketing. Marketing simply introduces the book to the market. If that manages to draw a potential customer close enough to take a look, then all well and good, but that is all it can do. If that person goes on to buy that book, it's simply because of a natural conjunction between the book's content and their currant need or desire. Marketing can only do so much. Selling is the art of creating a need or desire where it doesn't exist, or reinforcing where it exists but not firmly enough to convert into a sale.

Consider these two questions.

Does the owner of a bookshop, with a stock of books running into thousands, need to purchase yet another book to add to their huge stock?

Does an individual that enjoys reading need to

purchase your book more than any of the many thousands of other books they have to choose from?

Selling is the art of telling them that they need to buy your book. Closing the sale is the art of ensuring they do buy your book. And a salesperson doesn't wait for marketing to draw in a potential customer. A salesperson goes out hunting for their potential customer. Marketing is just waffle.

Selling is an art. It is a skill. It is a game with clearly established rules. It comes more naturally to some than to others, but it's not that difficult and anyone can learn.

To begin, have you ever wondered how, whenever you encounter someone trying to sell something, that they seem to have an answer for any objection you make?

The answer is, because sales people have a script and this script will contain rebuttals. A rebuttal is a reply to whatever objection to buying the product that the customer comes up with. These objections have been collected since the first Stone Age sales person started selling flint axe heads and now there is no objection to buying that hasn't been heard, collated and a host of replies developed to counter that objection.

Depending on the product, the script can be used almost verbatim, like performing a Shakespeare play, or as a guide, more ad-lib, only to fall back on if required. Some employ the real hard sell tactics, usually reserved for high cost items such as double-glazing, where there can be real sales resistance. Then tricks are employed, like the cup of tea/coffee trick, or the telephone close.

The tea/coffee trick comes into play when invited into someone's home to demonstrate, usually, some high value home improvement product. Being polite, the customer offers a cup of tea or coffee and the sales person always accepts no matter how many cups they've drunk that day. And after an hour or two, or more, the customer has made all their objections and had them countered and obviously wants the salesperson to leave and seeing the customer fidget, on the verge of demanding they leave, the salesperson picks up the cup and takes another sip of the long cold, foul tasting tea or coffee, knowing that most people are polite and won't insist they leave before finishing the drink they so innocently offered on arrival. And it is in to the next round.

The telephone close is another trick where the sales person, after continual objections, some excuse is made to phone the office and low and behold, by some miraculous reason, the customer can have the product at a vastly reduced price, but only if they buy then and there. This is miraculous because it happens even when the salesperson ends up speaking to an answering machine, or the speaking clock.

Thankfully these tricks don't apply when selling books, but you still begin with a script. The script starts with such basic things such as 'good morning/

afternoon and the one thing any good salesperson knows is that whatever the product, the first thing they sell is themself.

Selling involves an understanding of psychology and part of this psychology is the knowledge that people buy from people they like. Conversely, they don't buy from people they don't like. So you need to sell yourself as efficient, professional, personable, which means dressing the part and being fully prepared both in understanding what you are about to do and having everything you need to achieve what you need to do.

Part of this professionalism is to know the two different methods through which products are sold; direct selling and trade selling. Direct selling is exactly what it says, the manufacturer sells direct to the customer. Trade selling involves intermediaries such as distributors, retailers etc.

In trade selling, the price of any product is set using two different methods. With some products the manufacturer sets a wholesale price giving a recommended retail mark-up to whatever the retail price should be. With other products, the manufacturer sets a retail price, giving a trade discount on this recommended retail price. Books are sold using this second method and quoting a wholesale price expecting a bookseller to mark-up will show you up as not knowing the business. I say this because some self-publishers have done just this.

Another element of professionalism is to know what you are going to say and there is nothing worse than standing, facing someone and not knowing what to say. Even professional actors have been known to freeze when facing an audience so don't think it can't happen to you. Having a script will give you confidence and it doesn't have to be complicated. Simply think through what you intend to say before hand. If you have never done anything like this before, I recommend you practice in front of a mirror or go through a few sessions of role-play with a friend. Professional sales people with years of experience still do this at various sales training seminars because they accept the simple fact that if you get it wrong, you can't go back and do it over again. You've lost the sale and that's the end of it.

A good salesperson doesn't need to stick verbatim to the script. It is more of a guide, to ensure every point is covered. Remember that when negotiating a sale, you are in effect negotiating a legal contract. What you say and even what you don't say is important.

Another element of this is that the person you are trying to sell to is in business. They will be busy and have granted you a few moments of their busy schedule, so don't waste their time. The last thing they need is someone waffling around and around in circles.

Your script will start with such basics as good morning/afternoon and professionally written, will include the word *smile* in brackets alongside this because your expression is important.

Whether you've phoned beforehand and made an appointment, or it's a cold call, one where no appointment is made, you will commonly find that you will have to wait. Whatever you do, do not allow a look of impatience or frustration to cross your face. When you do get to see someone, they will likely apologise. Tell them it doesn't matter, and mean it, even if the delay has made you late for another appointment. Use the time to phone and apologise to whomever that may be.

You can also use this time to go fishing. By this I mean, look around the store. Look at what's on their shelves and where. This will indicate what sells and what doesn't. Look at their footfall. You can pick up a host of hints by just looking. Then, after saying that being kept waiting doesn't matter, offer some blandishment about their store. Make some positive comment because everyone likes praise, but don't go overboard. The buyer will be able to spot bullshit the minute it's said.

As stated, selling involves psychology. People buy from people they like and don't buy from people they don't like, so be likeable.

The Book Trade System

The book trade operates as a market chain. Publishers publish and sell to a book distributor. This book distributor sells to the bookshop. Bookshops come in two-forms, the independent and the chain. Then there are other outlets such as supermarkets and special interest retailers that take books on subjects within their specialist field. Behind these there is another link in the chain, the remainder dealer.

All publishers have lemons, a book produced with high expectations but didn't sell, or didn't sell in the volume expected. Unlike subsidy/vanity publishers with their pulping and other get out clauses, publishers print and bind books. Books that don't sell are sold off to the Remainder Trade in the hope of recouping the cost of production.

Remainder dealers also purchase mass-market copies of previous published and classic titles. These are produced by trade publishers who rarely, if ever, publish a previously unpublished title, yet they still receive submissions from authors who don't research before posting off their manuscript.

The book trade also operates a system called, Sale or Return. The shop agrees to stock your book on the condition that the publisher, after a set period of time, takes back any unsold copies, at no cost to the bookseller. The publisher takes the risk, though often giving the bookseller a smaller discount, maybe 20% instead of 35%, than if taken in the normal way.

Note that all discounts are subject to negotiation so before going in, you need to know how far you can go and this is where having a script plays another role. You will know that on a strait sale order of up to a certain value, you can give, for example a 35% discount. Over that value and to another set limit, you can allow up to 40% discount. Over yet another value, you can allow 50%, all subject to negotiation.

If, on the other hand, the buyer requires sale or return, you'll be working on a different level of discounts that you will know and have prepared beforehand. Having these facts and figures to hand is all part of appearing professional and professionalism counts. It is part of selling yourself and even if this is the first time you've entered the lion's den, the appearance of professionalism will still count.

Part of this professionalism is preparation. I know of several self-publishing authors that have gone into a bookshop and the owner has agreed to stock a few copies, but the author didn't have anything on which to write the order.

It doesn't take long to design and print an order form with your publisher name, address and contact information at the top and boxes beneath to fill in the customer's details and below that, boxes for the title, ISBN number, quantity, price, discount etc. Remember that the buyer will want a copy for their records. You can print your own along with old-fashioned carbon paper or use a printing service to create a professional looking duplicate pad. At the bottom of the sheet will be a place for their signature, because this is a legal contract. You supply, they purchase.

As for payment, don't expect payment then and there. It does happen, on small orders, but standard practice is to take the order, deliver, which you can then and there if you have the books in the boot of your car, then send an invoice, to be paid within 35 days of the invoice date.

These delivery costs, postage, paperwork, are all things you will have allowed for right at the start of the process, because they are all part of being a real publisher.

HOW TO SELL

Selling into multinational chains involves a subtly different approach from selling into small independent retail outlets. I'll deal with selling into independent outlets first.

Whether you've made an appointment or a cold call, it's the same process. Walk in, smile and ask for the manager/owner. The best way to do this is go up to the first person you see who is related to the business, even if they are obviously one of the most junior members of staff, and ask,

'Excuse me. Are you the owner/manager.'

You ask because there is no point in trying to sell to some junior that doesn't have the power to order. You'll just look a fool and have to repeat yourself all over again, if and when you do find the right person.

You ask if they are the owner/manager rather than just asking for the owner/manager because assuming that person is just a shop assistant can result in an unfortunate mistake, because they could be in charge. If they are what they appear to be, assuming they could be in charge will give their ego a boost and you've made a friend. You've sold yourself and they'll like you. They might even make a positive comment on what you are trying to sell. I've known many small business owners that have asked their staff if they think a book will sell and a positive comment can swing a sale.

When you find the right person, introduce yourself, giving your first name and last, not I'm Mr or Mrs ***. Offer to shake their hand, unless they have a hand full of books. They will probably take you into their office. Get out your order form and put it on the desk/counter. Think positive. Now continue.

*'I represent **** Books,'* whatever your imprint name might be.

'We're a small independent publisher set up to promote a number of exciting new authors.'

Using the plural, the royal 'we' sounds so much better and more professional than, 'I've just self published my first book and…" It is also justifiable because you've probably got a partner who's put up with all the time you've devoted to writing and getting your first book into print, along with the financial investment etc.

Note that most buyers started their career as a seller and will spot this sort of blarney, bull sh** whatever you want to call it, a mile away. They know it for what it is, but it is part of a pro-former process, as in politics, where people say what is expected. The one thing you must never ever do is tell a blatant untruth, because that will also be spotted for what it is.

Now, as at this stage, you will most likely only have a single title to sell, you follow the statement about being a small indie publisher with the line:

'The first of which is...'

Give the book's title. Refrain from saying you are the author. They might make the connection by connecting the author name on the cover and the name you gave when you introduced yourself; so use this as a positive.

'Yes. Certainly. But I didn't want to go down the self-publishing route, which is why I decided to set up my own independent publishing company and do things properly.'

Everyone in the book trade knows the difference between self-publishing, vanity publishing, indie publishing and mainstream publishing. There are certain publisher names that no book-seller will touch, whatever the offer, simply because they have a reputation as a vanity publisher, so you don't have to explain more. Silence is golden. Shut up. I'll cover this in a moment.

Wait to see what comment they make, if any. Play it by ear. You can't script everything, but you can work out what to say beforehand in response to whatever they might say next.

The statement above also carries a double subliminal message. It says you'll understand if they do not take your book while asking them to give a fellow small business a little leeway

While saying this I will have handed them a sample of the book/books I'm trying to place. The rule is, get a book into their hands. With experience you can read the expression on their face, telling whether they like the title, the cover illustration, the feel of the book.

'As you see, it's priced competitively for the market and we're doing a lot of promotion. There's going to be an article in the local paper/an interview on local radio.'

Note that everything you say must be true.

THEN SHUT UP.

The problem with a lot of sales people is that they don't know when to shut up. Silence is the golden tool of a good salesperson. You've made your pitch, the first to speak often wins the day.

Another fault is being so tied up in what you intend to say that you don't listen to what the potential buyer is saying, or failing to reply to any questions they might ask. This is not hard selling, where the sales person has to brow beat the customer into buying some useless piece of junk. This is trade selling. A negotiation. It is business and being a new publisher with a one off new book by an unknown author, you need an edge and very often the potential customer will give you that edge in what they are saying.

Within moments of making my opening introduction, I had a potential customer mumble, half to themselves, that if might be a good idea to stock something by a local author. The rest of the planned pitch went out of the window and I went straight to the close.

I said, *'Ok. I can let you have a dozen copies now and I'll tell you what, I'll hold back the invoice for an additional 30 days.'* Then I shut up. Silence reigned. Time 30 seconds of silence in a conversation and it seems a long time, but I'd made my offer. They can answer yes or no. It's in the balance. Selling is a numbers game. Some you win, some you loose, but the more you play the more you win. It's simply the rule of percentages.

So on a cold call, in a shop I'd never been in before, to a customer I'd never met, I sold a dozen copies on a firm sale without having to fall back and offer sale or return.

With experience, you can judge their reaction. At this point it's not what they say, but how they act. They might put the sample book down. If they push it away from them, that's a negative. If they leave it in place, that's a positive. They will be thinking. People don't like to be interrupted when thinking and I'm certainly not going to ask whether they'll place an order or not. Asking gives them the opportunity to say no. The trick is to sense the mood. I might add,

'Of course this is a new book by a new author so I can offer an additional thirty days before invoicing.'

The normal period for paying is 30 days from the date of the invoice, so you're saying they can have this book on their shelf for 60 days before paying the invoice. The important thing is to get your book on the shelf, where it stands a chance of being bought. Or I might say,

'I can put you down for six and still give you standard discount despite it being a small order.'

There is a trick in selling of only asking positive questions. These are questions where the answer is more likely to be 'yes', or where the question leans towards a 'yes' answer. Negative questions are avoided, as are, as far as possible, questions where the answer could be yes or no. The nature of questions is decided while writing the sales script, a task I have done for a number of different companies. Some sales scripts even include the instruction that the salesperson should nod heir head very slightly whenever they ask one of these questions. A nodding head indicates 'yes', an affirmative. You might think it silly, but selling is all about psychology and involves a lot of subliminal messaging. And it works.

Closing the Sale

Closing the sale is the most important part of the process. This is where the salesperson asks whether or not the customer is going to buy, except a good salesperson will never ask because it can result it a no answer. One way around this is to say,

'I've actually got a stock in the car so I can let you have them now, which will correspond with the promotion we're doing. Would five copies (of each) be

enough or would you rather take ten?

Of course they can still say no and if so, except with good grace. This is not the hard sell, where you use rebuttals to their objections. I've had shops turn me down on the first visit only to buy on the second. Plus, all selling is a numbers game. You won't sell all of the time, but see enough people and you will sell enough of the time.

So what if they ask about sale or return?

Asking is a sign that they are willing to take your book. Refusing will indicate that you are not confident that your book will sell. You prepare for this as well, don't bother. The correct action is to ask if you can leave 20 or more and make a good display of it.

As an anecdote, I once walked into what looked like a small independent that turned out to be part of a local chain, all with different names and no obvious linkage. The question was how many books they needed to order to get 40% discount because they'd then stock each shop. You prepare beforehand. You prepare what you are going to say, consider any questions you may be asked and be ready with the answers. You know how many books you want them to order to give what discount. If you know this you will be able to negotiate a deal.

The above is just an example of some of the script points you can use. Carry more than one pen. Carry a calculator. What is £8.99 x 5 - 35%? The key is to be prepared and to be as business like and as professional as you can be. Then you will sell.

Book Distributors

Major chains, such as Waterstones, require that all books they stock come through one of the major distributors. The Waterstones website even has a link that describes how to contact distributors such as Gardners, Bertrams etc. Something you might not know is that Gardners and a few other distributors also provide a POD service. For this, Gardners require that you be a publisher with a minimum of 5 titles in print.

Each distributor will have individual requirements and these can vary depending on the nature of the book in question. There will be basic requirements such as being able to provide the stock volume they require within the time limit they require it. Major distributors will also require a minimum 50-55% discount on the retail price of your book, something to consider when determining the production method for your book.

The simple fact is that many of the highly advertised *'self-publishing'* service cannot meet this requirement and is one of the main reasons their books never appear on the shelf any retail outlet. Instead of falling for the bright, flashy promises they offer, consider a company such as Clays Ltd (clays.co.uk), a book production company that produces books for major publishers such as Penguin. While this may appear beyond league of the small independent, the company readily deals with many small independent publishers. There is even a link on their website direct to the services they provide the small publisher. Companies like Clays also provide a direct link into the major distributor supply chain. Of course you will need to register your publisher information with that supply chain, the knock on effect being reduced delivery costs. Your book will be just one title amongst a whole truckload of different titles being delivered at the same time. In business, every angle needs to be considered, weighed and a judgement made.

While you are looking for quotes for the production of your book, you really need to think outside the box. For example, you could consider companies like China Printing Solutions, to name just one. Of course this means a larger print run, but labour costs are cheaper and labour costs are a major element in the cost of doing anything, even with the cost of shipping added. The result being that you get a far greater number of books for the same cost, meaning a lower per book production cost, meaning you can easily meet the 55% discount required by any major distributor.

Selling to Libraries

Selling to libraries is something a great many self-publishers hesitate to even attempt, but there are a number of benefits. Doing it will help establish you as an author and can lead to further sales, plus there is the potential for earnings through the public lending rights system.

Public Lending Rights (PLR), in the U.K. is the right for authors, illustrators and other contributors to receive payments based on the loan data collected from a sample selection of public libraries.

The U.K. PLR is administered by the British Library from the PLR Office, British Library, Stockton on Tees. For further information and to download an application form to register for PLR, contact the PLR Office on-line.

Before that you will need to get your book into the library system. To do this you could go through one of the major wholesalers, Gardners, Askews and Bertrams in the U.K. that sell to libraries, or do it yourself. Luckily you will not need to contact each individual library as there is usually one point of contact for each region, usually called the Library Acquisitions Officer and often based at the central or main reference library of each region. Each library region has its own website so the correct point of contact is not too difficult to research.

At the very least, your book must have an ISBN number and be registered with the relevant ISBN Agency. At one time libraries only took case bound books but now stock Paperbacks, mainly because they cost less to purchase. As well as the ISBN number, it benefits if your book is also registered with the Bibliographic Data Service (BDS). To register at BDS, visit http:www.bibliographicdata.co.uk/.

When approaching a library to sell your book, everything I've said about selling still applies. Make sure you use each and every selling point, such as any local connections within the story or any other local angle. Sometimes the library will agree to purchase your book, but wish to do so through one of the major wholesalers they usually deal with. The wholesaler may then approach you seeking to purchase and stock your book resulting in further sales to their other customers, which is probably the biggest benefit of all from trying to break into the library system.

The Remainder Trade

But now you are worried about being left with an unsold stock of books. All publishers' worry about this and all publishers have lemons; the book produced with high expectations that didn't sell, or didn't sell in the volume expected. Unlike subsidy/vanity publishers with a pulping and other get out clauses, publishers print and bind books. Books that don't sell are sold off to the Remainder trade in the hope of recouping the cost of production.

The Remainder trade are distributors and outlets set up specifically to take remainders, the unsold book stock that is then sold at a discount. The Remainder trade also purchase the rights to previously published titles and re-publish these titles as cheaply as possible, for sale through their own and other low cost outlets.

Note that Remainder trade publishers do not publish new and previously unpublished titles, yet they still receive submissions from authors who fail to research the publisher requirements before posting off their manuscript.

Remainder dealers such as Ciana (ciana.co.uk) even hold Remainder trade book fairs. These fairs are for trade only and proof of being in the book trade is required before being able to attend. Another company, Ziffit, (ziffit.com) provide an online outlet for unwanted book stock.

Note that the mention of any company is not a recommendation for the services they provide. Their names are given for information only.

Direct Selling

Ok, now let's go back to starting small. Direct selling is exactly what it says on the tin, direct selling from the producer to the end user. The benefit is that it cuts out the middleman and any share of the profit they might take. The drawback is that you have to do it all yourself.

The point to note here is that you can only do it yourself if you have a stock of books to sell. This strikes out print on demand. Print on demand is only viable for online sales, where it can be very good and does negate a high upfront cost. E publishing is also ruled out because that relies on a computer download system linked to some form of e-reader. Short run printing is the best option and because your not selling through the trade, you can get away with DIY produced books that may have minor, but not obvious, faults.

Now I've often heard self-publishers complain about being left with a stock of books cluttering up their garage, or shed, or spare room. Sorry. No sympathy. Those books are only cluttering up your garage, shed or spare room because those authors haven't got out there and sold those books, and don't say they won't sell. You can sell anything.

There is the well-known selling story of the salesman that went out and sold refrigerators to Eskimos. Alaska is permanently cold, so why would the Inuit, Tlingit or any of the other generally called Eskimo people need a refrigerator? Because where they live is permanently cold. It is so cold that their food is frozen and they need to thaw it out before they can cook it. A working fridge is insulated to keep the cold in, but to keep the cold out. Food kept in the fridge doesn't freeze so is ready to cook. Problem solved. It's all a matter of finding the angle.

Do you've got a stock of books to sell. If you need to, stick up a big sign saying SALE, or REDUCED. There are people out there who see a SALE sign and go into a trance. (Don't mention the wife). They don't see the item. They see is that it's reduced and therefore believe they are saving money.

Psychology again. It is why products are priced at, for example £7.99. People see the seven pounds and don't work out that it's only a penny below eight pounds.

In direct selling, you are selling direct to the customer, so don't need to give 35% or even 50% of the price to some retail outlet. So you have this to play with, but if you are giving a discount, make a big play of it. Tell people how much they are saving by buying now.

As for those people that complain they've got a stack of books in their garage, I've got no sympathy because they can be sold, it only takes a bit of effort. If needed, they can sell at cost. As a last resort they can be sold at a loss, enough to recoup some of the production costs. There is no excuse for not selling – anything.

Finding Customers?

Start with the hardest. You can go from door to door, not asking people if they want to buy your book because that opens the way for a no answer. You tell them you have published this book and feel sure they'll be interested while pushing it into their hand. Sell yourself. Don't tell them how much it is. Wait for them to ask, because asking is a sign they're interested in buying. Then prefix whatever price it is with the word 'only' while watching for any hesitation or equivocation. Learn to read body language. See this and jump in and say something like, *'You can have this book now for nearly half the price you'd pay in a shop.'*

All selling is a numbers game and there's a virtual guarantee that in any street of 50 houses you will sell at least 1 copy. It is a basic selling statistic that you will sell to a percentage of the calls you make. Make the calls and you <u>will</u> sell. Don't make the calls and you won't. It's a simple as that. Now let's look at some easier options.

But there is an easier way to sell.

Book fairs are one, but don't just think of the large annual book fairs full of established authors and publishers and agents all hyping their latest books. There are often local and regional fairs and also second hand and collectable book selling events. And not just book fairs. Any fete, function, event open day, where the organisers are offering traders the opportunity pitch a stand or rent a table, provides an opportunity to sell. The benefit of attending such events is that the people that go there are generally in the mood to buy. Selling is all about understanding psychology and people go to such events in a relaxed mood and generally with the expectation that they will need to spend some money.

I sell books at Christmas markets, because a book is a great, low cost present for that distant aunt or uncle, or cousin, to whom you're expected to give a present but don't want to spend too much. I've sold books at local farmer's markets. I've sold books on a beach. There is nowhere you can't sell and no excuse for not selling.

You'll need a poster, some sort of sign to say why you're there. Have a stack of 4 or 5 books, not too many, not too few. Stand one up on display. Take some business cards as well with your name, job description as AUTHOR in big letters, plus your contact details. If you find someone interested, you don't want to be scrabbling around for a piece of paper on which to write your name and number. As with trade selling, you'll want a script so you know what to say. And don't just stand there like a lemon waiting for anyone that glances your way to speak. Watch for anyone showing the slightest interest and first, sell yourself. Smile. Psychology again. A smile says you're friendly. A grimace says, go away. Say something, anything. Saying good morning/afternoon only is too bland. It might elicit a response but it doesn't lead anywhere, so ask a question instead or as well. *'Good morning. Are you enjoying the fair/fete/whatever?'*

This requires an answer. Now you've initiated a conversation. *'I'm here promoting my knew book.'* Don't say *'selling'* because that tells them you want to sell you're book. Psychology again. They will know that is what you want to do, but the thought is in the back of their mind. It's not prominent. Mention the word *'selling'* and it will bring it to the front of their mind with big flashing lights with bells on.

The trick is that when saying that you are there promoting your new book, and again, psychology plays a role, saying *'your new book'* hints that there are others even if it's the only one. This helps sell the image of you being an established writer. So you are there to promote your new book and while saying it, you proffer one with the obvious intention that they take it to have a look. Most people will instinctively take it. So now they've got a book in their hand, so they can't walk off without giving it back and your hands are down by your sides well away from indicating that you are ready to take it back. So they are now effectively your captives.

Now you want a USP. A unique selling point. Why should they be interested? Perhaps the book is set in the local area or has some local connection. Non-fiction is easier in some ways, because it relates to specific interests, harder in others, because you need to find a potential buyer with that interest. If your book is about hot air ballooning and you're at a hot air balloon festival, that's not a problem, but if it's about hot air ballooning and you're at a steam rally, its another matter.

So you've accosted your potential customer and they've got a book in their hand and now they're beginning to realise that you're trying to sell them something and the first objection is coming into their head, so throw them a curve ball. *'Do you live locally?'*

Mentally they are saying, *what? Eh?* Objection forgotten. They ill probably mumble an affirmative or somewhere nearby. If they say they're on holiday, ask where from. Wherever that is there may be something in the novel that connects. If not, it doesn't matter. If there is a connection, use it.

'That's a coincidence. This book is set around here/there. The hero is a local man. It's based around a historical battle set near here.' Any link you can find is an angle you can use to maintain and grow interest. Of course there may not be any link at all. No matter. As with selling fridges to Eskimos, flexibility is the key, or you could get straight to the point. In fact you don't want to waste too much time because they might not buy and while you are talking, other people are walking past, maybe stopping for a look but getting away because you are talking to someone else. So there is a judgement call to make. If they seem interested, carry one. If they are fidgeting, looking around, or giving off any other signal that they are looking for an excuse to escape, let them go. *'Say, well nice talking to you.'* Take the book back and target the person looking at the book on the table.

Or you can simply say, *'This is my new book and it's available at a special promotion price because of the fete/fair/whatever.'*

Note you haven't told them the price. Psychology again. You want them to ask because asking the price is a signal that they are thinking of buying. You can tell them or you can use a classic distraction trick. After making the above statement, or after they ask the price, you say something like: *'Having a good day out?'* or *'Are you enjoying whatever.'* Wait for their answer. Then go back. *'The book, it's only £X.99.'* If you are selling at something .99p always make sure you have lots of pennies for change because you will sell.

I often take my wife and kids to such events. When they are not looking around, they keep the potential customer's partner occupied, meaning the customer can't get away. I'll always let them go if they genuinely show no interest. I might counter a few objections, but never browbeat or hard sell. I also read as well, so take a stock of second hand books. In addition I produce books for a few other authors so take a stock of these as well. This gives me more to sell than just a single title, adding to the attraction to draw people in. Selling is a numbers game and if you talk to enough people, you are virtually guaranteed to sell.

SUMMARY

The first thing to do is avoid all those companies that advertise and phone and e-mail wanting to publish your book. What they really want is for you to pay them to publish your book.

If you are determined to publish your own book, approach the project as would any other mainstream publisher. This means gaining a knowledge and understanding of the potential market before you begin.

Knowing the market will guide you to the level of potential sales. Knowing this will guide you to the best method and format in which to publish your book, allowing you to decide the size of print run and determine the best per book cost to allow when producing your book.

Now we have the issue of editing. It is very difficult to self edit your own book simply because of a natural tendency to look at the process from the perspective of a writer. To illustrate the problem, this book is self-edited and there are probably some mistakes that I have failed to spot. I could argue that this is deliberate, to illustrate just how difficult it is to self edit. After all, a book such as this, especially a book such as this, shouldn't contain mistakes. I do a lot of editing, of other people's work, and find it far easier to spot those mistakes than my own, so if there is one thing you should pay out for, it's editing. The chapters in this book only give a brief summary on what to look for.

Learning to design and layout your own book opens any number of avenues for production. Physical books are laid out using a DTP application and then converted to PDF. Most E-book providers offer templates to suit their system, meaning you can upload from Word or any other word processing application, but an understanding of the principles of book layout is still a benefit so well worth doing.

As for going the whole hog and printing, using a good quality digital duplex laser printer, binding using a desktop binding system and trimming using a ream cutter or guillotine, it's not impossible. Admittedly it is more viable for books with a low sales target, or even where sales are expected to be slow, or seasonal, selling over a long period of time, but take into account that a great many self published books have a sales target of 100 to become a best seller and doing it this way becomes a viable option.

Whatever method you choose, the only way to publish your own book is to become a publisher. This is easy enough to achieve and there are hurdles to overcome. I hope I've explained the hurdles, not to make the process appear difficult, but to describe how they can be overcome.

You then move to the design and production stage and again, there are hurdles to overcome. Not one of them is too high or too difficult to deal with, but they must be dealt with, in order and with precision. Yes you can publish your own book, but it's all about doing it properly. Do it properly and there is a chance of success. There is no guarantee, other than not doing it properly is a virtual guarantee of failure.